SHARING
THE LIGHT

SHARING
THE LIGHT

IN THE WILDERNESS

FAVORITE TALKS FROM ESPECIALLY FOR YOUTH

Deseret Book Company
Salt Lake City, Utah

Library of Congress Cataloging-in-Publication Data.

Sharing the light in the wilderness : favorite talks from Especially
  for youth.
     p. cm.
   Summary: A collection of essays using a Mormon perspective to view
  such topics as family life, dating, living the Word of Wisdom, and
  relationships.
   ISBN 0-87579-717-2 (soft cover)
    1. Teenagers — Religious life — Juvenile literature. 2. Teenagers —
Conduct of life — Juvenile literature. 3. Church of Jesus Christ of
Latter-day Saints — Doctrines. 4. Mormon Church — Doctrines.
[1. Christian life. 2. Conduct of life. 3. Church of Jesus Christ
of Latter-day Saints — Doctrines. 4. Mormon Church — Doctrines.]
BX8643.Y6S53   1993
248.8'3 — dc20   93-2985
                                                                     CIP
                                                                      AC

Printed in the United States of America
10   9   8   7   6   5   4   3   2   1

CONTENTS

COVENANT RELATIONSHIPS THAT COUNT

SCOTT L. ANDERSON

Mark was about the most pleasant young man anyone could meet. He constantly smiled, and radiated concern for others, and showed true friendship. That's why his friends encouraged him to run for student-body president. His narrow defeat (by only eleven votes) to a good friend seemed only to enhance his positive outlook and charismatic personality. When he ran for senior-class president, he won easily, and his warmth and sense of humor helped make the year memorable. In time his mission call came, and off he went to serve his Heavenly Father — making an offering of all his admirable qualities to the Lord. Then came the leukemia, a trip home to seek medical treatment, and a courageous return to the mission field in an attempt to complete his assignment. He wasn't able. Mark's cancer was not curable. He passed away at age twenty.

Think with me for a moment. If Mark could get permission to return to mortality for just five minutes, what do you suppose he would he say to us? Would he say that his greatest accomplishment was being elected a class officer in high school? Would he tell us that dating was the highlight of his life? Would he even say that friends mattered most? I think that one of the central messages he would deliver would be to strengthen the "covenant relationships" in our lives — our family relationships.

How much time do we spend thinking of our someday-dream-companion? How much energy and money do we expend hoping and preparing for "Mr. Right" or "Miss Marvelous" to come into our lives? But, what about the other eternal relationships in our lives—Mom and Dad, brothers and sisters? That may make you uneasy. You are probably thinking, "Eternity is a long time! Will my brother still be the major eternal tease of the next life? Will I have to put up with my sister borrowing my clothes forever? And will my parents still be telling me what time to come in at night when I come home from the next galaxy?"

Of course we know that many things will be different there, but shouldn't we spend a portion of the time, effort, and money we use up in the dating scene (trying to find an eternal companion) to strengthen the eternal relationships that have already been established?

Does that mean you have to double-date with your parents every other Friday? No. But it might be fun sometimes, because they usually will pay the bill! Let's see what the scriptures tell us about strengthening family relationships.

THE NEPHI EXPERIENCE

You have probably read the story of how Nephi left Jerusalem with his family to journey to the promised land. In fact, you have probably read it many times, because this story comes before the Isaiah chapters in the Book of Mormon, and they make a lot of people stop reading and start the book over.

One time our family decided to try to duplicate what it was like for Nephi and his family. I got home from work on a typical Monday afternoon, and walked in the house to find my children seated in a row. They had bandannas tied around their heads and puzzled looks on their faces.

"So, what's up?" I asked.

They replied, "Dad, Mom's being weird!"

Just then, out of the corner of my eye, I noticed my wife descending the stairs with a bow and an arrow in one hand and a bandanna in the other—obviously for me.

"So, what's going on?" I asked again.

She said, "Come, we're going to the wilderness!"

We all marched out into the backyard and into the trees beyond, where a boldly lettered sign was displayed—THE WILDERNESS—so we knew we had arrived.

As we sat down, my wife inquired, "What if we never went home again?"

The "Tank," my seven-year-old (whose first word in this life was "food"), said, "I'll starve to death!"

Mom retorted, "Oh no. Dad brought his bow and arrow, and you will be just fine."

The Tank looked skeptical and replied, "Oh yes we will starve. I don't think he knows how to use it!"

"What do we need to take with us, if we are never going to go home again?" Mom asked. The children began making their lists. We quickly found out that girls pack differently for an extended vacation than boys do. But, if I had read my scriptures more carefully, I would have already known this. In his account, Nephi explains that as they left Jerusalem, his family consisted in part of Laman, Lemuel, and Sam, and that they took provisions and tents and departed. (See 1 Nephi 2:4–5.) Sounds like boys going on a scout camp. No curling irons, make-up, and so on.

However, Ishmael's family (many daughters) was different. The scriptures tell us that Ishmael and his entire "household" took their journey into the wilderness! (See 1 Nephi 7:5.) We found this true in our little family—the boys' lists were brief but my daughters'—oh boy!

Finally, my oldest daughter mentioned that we would need to take our scriptures. (We give away double refreshment coupons for correct FHE answers.)

"Right answer!" I declared. "Who will go and get the scriptures?"

Jonathan jumped up and said, "I will, if I can go by the fridge!"

He returned with an Old Testament wrapped in tin foil that said "Brass Plates" on the front.

Seeing him approach, my wife exclaimed, "Here comes Nephi!"

"Nope," he said, "it's only Jonathan."

"Well, you look like Nephi."

"Oh, yeah? Well, what does he look like?"

"He's tall, and strong, and handsome, and powerful, and good."

"Yup. That's me!"

We then talked about having a "Nephi-attitude" — being willing, and not complaining — as opposed to a "Laman-and-Lemuel-attitude." (We shortened it to a "lemon" attitude.) The only time those two *didn't* complain was when they were asked to go back for Ishmael's daughters!

We then "slept" for a couple of minutes and awakened to find the "Liahona" in our camp. It was an automotive wax can, wrapped in tin foil, closed with a transparent lid, and with a message inside. (I hope that's not sacrilegious, but it *was* of "curious workmanship.")

It gave directions which we followed and we found ourselves at a table filled with the children's favorite kinds of foods. My wife informed them that if they'd follow the real Liahona (the Holy Ghost) in their lives they would find even better food than this. We took turns "hunting" with the bow and arrow, and ended up at home again.

At this point in our "lesson" I wanted to see what we had learned, so I said, "Act like Laman and Lemuel for a minute." (There is no need to ask for this — kids act like this naturally.)

Before they went too far, I begged, "Act like Nephi and Sam!"

They replied, "Great, Dad. Fantastic, Father. Whatever you say."

Then I asked the important question: "Who do you want to be like?"

They replied, "Nephi and Sam." (Of course they gave the correct answer, because they knew we would go back to the wilderness and do it all over again if they got it wrong!)

A closing prayer, and the activity was over. But the application was just beginning. As I started to clean up the "wilderness," I asked if anyone wanted to help. The "Tank" jumped up and exclaimed, "Great, Dad! Just like Nephi, huh!"

This activity started a tradition that has gone on for many

years in our family. For instance, my "tank" of a son now plays college football. (I often just salute him, and ask him if he needs more money.) He still says, "Great, Dad," with a "Nephi" twinkle in his eye when I ask him to do something. When I recently ordained him an elder, it was obvious that his attitude extended to another Father, and that his desire was to say "Great, Father, whatever you say!"

I look forward to the day when I can personally thank Nephi for the difference he has made in our efforts to strengthen the eternal relationships in our family. When we need direction, our "Liahona" works best when we are willing to get along as a family. When we need to accomplish something as a family, we remember that Nephi and his family found success when they worked together as a team. Often, in the "wilderness of our afflictions," a Nephi-like-attitude has helped pull us through.

Mom and Dad

I recall the farewell sacrament meeting of a student of mine who was preparing to leave on his mission. In the meeting, his mother said her son was a true friend to the other members of their family, and described how he had been a great help to her in the home. She was fearful that it would take two people to replace him. While he was on his mission she *got* two people to replace him — she gave birth to twin boys.

A young woman stood at the door of her seminary class, greeting each student as they entered, and presenting each with a piece of candy. They all said, "Thanks," as they took their seats. The candy-giver was to lead the devotional that day. After the song and prayer, she issued this challenge: "Every one of you thanked me for the candy. Robin even gave me a hug. I spent sixty-five cents on this candy, and it was money that I borrowed. But think of what your parents have given and sacrificed. When was the last time you really thanked them, gave them a hug? You see, my mom died four months ago, and now I do all the meals and laundry and have a little idea how much of her life she sacrificed for me. If I could just have five minutes with her, I would thank her for all the daily things she did for us that I took for granted! Her great life was full of so much service."

It's not always easy to talk to your parents, though it is easier at some times than at others. I remember when I first learned that. My mom would almost always get in this crazy mood about 11:00 PM. It seemed at that time of night she would laugh at almost anything! We spent many nights sitting in front of the fireplace in her sitting room, laughing hysterically. If I ever had anything major to confess, it was accomplished best at 11:05 P.M. I would just get her laughing, then inform her, "I just wrecked the car!" and we would have a great chuckle. So, I guess the truth is out—parents are people! They can become our best friends. Sometimes I still call my mom at 11:05 at night when I want a good laugh and want to talk.

There are so many ways to support parents—even parents who aren't active in the Church, or even if they aren't all we'd like them to be. When things got tough in Nephi's family, and even Lehi was beginning to "murmur against the Lord his God," (1 Nephi 16:20), Nephi still went to his dad for direction. He could have decided that because his father was not as close to the Spirit as he should have been, it wouldn't be appropriate to seek his father's counsel. Nephi went to him anyway. He allowed his father to fill his rightful role in the family, and to properly exercise his priesthood.

During testimony meeting at EFY, a girl named Loni said, "I was listening to one of the speakers share the account of Nephi supporting his father during the time when Lehi was struggling. I couldn't help thinking of my own dad. He has been inactive for years, and I have often felt like I didn't have an obligation to support him. But, I really think that I can help him, too."

Next came a testimony from a young man who surprised the group by getting up. He said, "I don't even know why I'm here standing in front of you. I don't even think I have a testimony. But, when Loni was talking, I felt like I just wanted to do some-thing to help her. I felt that if everyone fasted for her this next Fast Sunday, that maybe things might work out better with her father." The tears came, and he stood quietly waiting for the ability to go on. Then he said, "I feel such a spirit right now—Heavenly Father is telling me that our united faith and prayers can really make a difference. I do feel like I know this gospel has the answers." It was a wonderful thing to be there and to see the Spirit work.

By the next day, we had all left to go home from EFY. We were all scattered, from the Marshall Islands to Florida, but that Sunday we all fasted for a beautiful sister and her father. Not long after that fast, the letter came. Loni had felt prompted to talk to her father the very day we were all fasting. Knowing that people all over the world were praying for her, gave her great courage. She had a wonderful talk with her father, and he attended a fireside with her that night to hear Howard W. Hunter speak. She had invited him to firesides for years, but he had not come. Tonight was different. Her excitement bounced off the pages of her letter. Her dad had actually attended a fireside with the family! Weeks later another letter arrived. Now her father had even attended church with the family. Who says that lives can't change! I testify there is power in fasting unitedly for an important cause—especially when families are in need. I know that youth can make a difference in their families.

In the Book of Mormon, Alma has a great talk with his son, Helaman (see Alma 36). In this discussion, Alma thanks Helaman for being such a great young man—so much stronger than Alma was as a youth. Their relationship seemed so close, and reading about it helped me realize that I had a great son myself, and that he was definitely better than I had ever been at his age. It occurred to me that I had seldom expressed that idea to him. When I got home that night, I called him into the study. We sat down to have a "man to man" talk. I tried to be like Alma and thank him for his great example, and then said, "I think you must have been my big brother in heaven." He agreed with me and exclaimed, "Dad, I've been thinking the same thing!"

You can make a great difference in your home! Having a Nephi-attitude is fun. Try it next time your mom asks you to get busy on the dishes. Say, "Sure, Mom. I'd love to!" You probably won't even have to do the dishes. She will faint, and you can get your little brothers and sisters to do the work before she wakes up! Another idea is to tell your parents that you need to interview them. Tell them that you are concerned about them: are they getting enough rest? keeping up with their chores? keeping their grades up? You can be the one to help open the door to communication with your parents.

Brothers and Sisters

I was at a testimony meeting recently and heard a wonderful young woman say that her brother had just received his mission call, and that she didn't know what she would ever do without him. She explained, "When I was twelve and thirteen years old, and fighting the pimples and struggling at school, my 'Mr. Cool' and 'awesome' high school brother would stop by my room each night and say things like, 'Kari, you are so beautiful. Thanks for being my sister!' " She went on to say that, had it not been for him, she didn't know how she would have made it through those difficult years.

Hearing her made me wonder what my brothers and sisters would have said about me. There were so many times I could have been a brother like that. I also long to have been more like my friend, who donated his kidney to his brother. Knowing that sometimes kidney transplants don't take, and that there was a possibility that the operation would be a failure, he had gladly given his organ anyway—to help save the life of the brother he loved. I often think about the many times my own brothers and sisters needed me, when I just wasn't sensitive to those needs. Although I wish I had been a better brother then, I have vowed to be a better one now.

LOVE BOX

Our family was sitting together during family home evening one night, when my wife displayed a beautifully wrapped box. It appeared that one of us was going to receive a gift. My wife announced that this box was called the "Love Box," and said, "There is nothing inside but love, and I would like to give it to

Janalyn." She walked over to our daughter, looked into her eyes, and said, "I love you so much. Thank you for helping with the little ones when I needed to talk with my upset friend the other day. You have a way of knowing just how to help best." The box was then given to Jana to pass on. "Nate," she said, "I love you. You always make me happy when I'm sad—especially when you climb up on my lap and give me a kiss. Thanks for being my little brother!" The box was passed around the whole family, and each member was the recipient of an expression of love.

There are hundreds of ways to share our love for our families. Notes left in secret, secret pals, quiet acts of service, taking our brothers and sisters along with a friend to an activity, taking the kids out and giving our parents some time for a date, visiting grandparents with our dates, to play games or just talk. Another idea is to get a "You're the Best" plate and set it at a family member's place on special days—or just any day. Spending time talking or laughing (at 11:05 PM)—schedule it in if you have to— will be worth it. Give that ol' "Nephi-attitude" a try—you may be surprised at the result.

I testify that, as President Benson has said, our youth are the spiritual stripling warriors of today. In the case of your counterparts, the stripling warriors of old, it was their families that prepared them to fulfill their destiny. (See Alma 56:47–48). It is important that you maintain your relationships with your parents and with your brothers and sisters. These covenant relationships deserve your greatest effort to build and maintain them. Our Father in Heaven wants us to succeed as families, and he will help us. I challenge you to think up better ways than ever before to show love in these relationships that are eternal.

Scott Anderson is an institute teacher at Utah Valley Community College in Orem, Utah. He enjoys construction work, sports, writing, and singing. Scott has traveled widely, visiting such countries as Egypt, Israel, Greece, Germany, and many others. Brother Anderson is a popular speaker at youth conferences. He and his wife, Angelle, have six children.

2

WHATEVER IT TAKES

ART E. BERG

The runners stood anxiously in the cool morning air, awaiting the sound of the gun that would signal the start of the race. The horizon glowed as the first rays of sunlight began to stretch across the sky. Conversation among the runners was subdued as each participant contemplated the miles ahead.

I sat quietly in my wheelchair, making the final adjustments necessary before the start of the race. This was my first race. Two years earlier I had broken my neck in an automobile accident that had made me a quadriplegic, and that had confined me permanently to a wheelchair. The doctors had told me again and again of the things I would never be able to do—things like participate in sports or athletic competition.

As a quadriplegic, I was paralyzed from the chest down. I had no use of my legs, stomach muscles, or of two of my major chest muscles. I had limited use of my shoulders and arms, no use of my right triceps, and I couldn't move my hands. To further complicate things, my body would no longer sweat, a condition that added the danger of heat stroke to athletic activities.

I had prepared for months for this five-mile race. The night before was nearly a sleepless one as I considered the challenge. What if couldn't finish? What if I got overheated? Why was I doing this? I knew the answer to the last question—I wanted to get better. I wanted to become independent again, and I hoped increasing my strength would help. Racing would give me a reason to train, and would provide me with a daily measure of my progress.

The moment came as the gun sounded and hundreds of runners shot forward. My glove quickly found the push ring, and I moved across the starting line. I soon found a steady pace which I felt I could maintain, and I began to focus my thoughts on the triumphant victory I would have as I crossed the finish line, perhaps forty minutes later.

Within minutes I was left alone as the last of the running pack rounded the first corner of the course and was lost from my view. I tried to quicken my pace for a time, but fatigue began to set in, and so I slowed to a more comfortable rhythm. As I reached the first mile marker, the empty water cups strewn across the road were evidence that I was still on the right path, although I could see no runners in the distance.

When I approached the second mile, the sun had risen higher in the sky, and my breathing became measurably heavier. My already slow, methodical pace grew even slower. Doubts began to enter my mind about whether I should be racing. I wondered if maybe the doctors were right after all.

The race involved several loops which brought the competitors near the finish line before the race was completed. The course design gave runners the option of quitting the race early if they were too exhausted, and returning to the starting/finish line. The last cutoff for making that decision was at the three-mile mark.

As I approached the three-mile marker, I stared toward the direction of the finish line. Most of the runners had long since finished. I had been on the road for more than an hour-and-a-half. My arms were tired, my breathing was labored, and my body temperature was rising. I had a decision to make . . . I was going forward.

With new resolve, I increased my pace. While the sun's heat was making my head feel light, I redoubled my determination. I could make it. I would finish — whatever it took. As I passed mile marker four, I stopped to pour some water on my head to lower my body temperature, before beginning the last stretch. As I drew closer to the finish line I continued to struggle. My arms felt like lead and my vision was blurry.

Rounding the final corner, I could see the finish line ahead. Other runners, who had long since finished their race, ran to my side to offer encouragement and hope. They shouted praise, and urged me forward. My face was wet with tears of exhaustion and desire as I slowly crossed the finish line and fell into my wife's arms, two-and-a-half hours after I started the race. I had done it.

Living requires us to make many decisions — small and large. In the end, our lives are the sum of our decisions. When we make poor decisions, based on either bad judgment, wrong information, or pride, we suffer a degree of pain and discomfort, and we lose a measure of happiness from our lives. When we make proper, good decisions, we find ourselves content and leading enriched and serene lives, even though we may not entirely escape the pains associated with this life.

When we make decisions, we commit ourselves to follow a certain path. However, as we move down the pathways of our new decisions, we sometimes begin to doubt ourselves and wonder about the direction we are going. Our commitment may begin to wane. When we have made poor decisions to begin with, this becomes a healthy process. However, it is destructive if we make decisions that draw us away from that which is good and right.

All of us have felt the stinging temptations of the Evil One as we have attempted to walk in the steps of the Savior. It suits Satan's purposes if we can be convinced we should take an easier, less righteous way, or abandon our resolve to live the commandments. Many things conspire to discourage us — perhaps we imagine we will lose friends, surrender popularity, or sacrifice opportunities. When we get into such a frame of mind, Satan quickly intrudes to attack our resolve, and we sometimes find ourselves making poor decisions, and suffering the attendant feelings of guilt, pain, and anguish.

Whenever we find ourselves experiencing pain, whether it is from unwise behavior, a poor relationship, or a struggling business, we can frequently trace the pain back to one key poor decision. Until one decides to do whatever it takes to be righteous, to achieve their dreams, to succeed in a relationship, there are doors opened for doubt, indecision, and hesitation. There is great power in making an absolute decision to do whatever it takes. Such resolve frustrates even Satan himself.

It has been my experience that when we decide to do whatever it takes, regardless of how difficult or hard the way may be, the Lord opens new ideas, opportunities, and paths for us to choose from—to make the way possible. As Nephi and his brothers made their way back to Jerusalem to retrieve the brass plates from Laban, Laman and Lemuel went along with only half their hearts. Sure, they had decided to go—a good decision—but they were not completely willing to do whatever it might take to accomplish their purpose. Perhaps they thought they would give it a try, while holding in their minds the option of bailing out if things got rough. However, we can never truly "give it our best shot," so long as we are waivering in our resolve.

Nephi, on the other hand, left himself with only one course of action—to do what the Lord commanded. He declared, "I will go and do the things which the Lord hath commanded, for I know that the Lord giveth no commandments unto the children of men, save he shall prepare a way for them that they may accomplish the thing which he commandeth them" (1 Nephi 3:7). Nephi aptly displayed his intentions when he stated, "As the Lord liveth, and as we live, we will not go down unto our father in the wilderness until we have accomplished the thing which the Lord hath commanded us" (1 Nephi 3:15). With that decision, absolute conviction, and commitment, the Lord opened a way for Nephi to complete the revealed task. A nation was saved because one man was willing to do whatever it takes.

Both converts and longtime members sometimes struggle with the commitment to obey the laws of God in exactness. Some find it difficult to change behavior, thoughts, and activities of the past, even while looking toward a new and brighter future within the gospel. Sometimes behavior changes for a time, but when temptations become too great, those who lack resolve slip back into old habits or make poor decisions.

King Lamoni's father followed the traditions and habits of his people. He lived a life that was far from that of a Christian. Yet, when he learned the truth, when the spirit bore witness to his heart of the reality of the gospel and the saving grace of Jesus Christ, he decided to change. But he did more than just decide, he committed himself totally to the path of righteousness and declared, "I will give up all that I possess, yea, I will forsake my kingdom, that I may receive this great joy. . . I will give away all my sins to know [him]" (Alma 22:15,18). And he did.

What are we willing to give away or to give up to know God? Are we willing to do whatever it takes? Or, are we only willing to be obedient as long as it is convenient?

"Yes, I'd be honored," was my answer to the question that had been cautiously asked by a member of my bishopric. He had asked me to become an early-morning seminary teacher. My wife, Dallas, stared at me with the thought clearly written in her eyes, "But, how?" The counselor smiled, thanked me, shook our hands, and informed me that my materials would be delivered later in the week. Shutting the door behind him, he was on his way.

Then Dallas asked the question that had been swirling in her mind. "How, Art? How are you going to do it?" My answer was less than comforting. I responded, "I don't know."

Having accepted the assignment, Dallas and I had some very real problems to solve. During the four years since my accident, dressing myself was something I had not been able to do. I had been informed by my doctors and therapists that I was going to have to depend on others for many things I would never be able to do for myself. They had advised me that because of having only limited use of my arms and hands, "You'll always need some-one to help you. Wherever you go, whatever you do, you'll never be fully independent again. Get used to it." And for four years I had struggled to find ways to help myself. I had learned to drive a van that was specially equipped to meet my needs, to get myself from place to place, to begin to earn an income, and to prepare my own meals. But one challenge seemed to defy a solution — I had not been able to dress myself.

"Yes" had been my response to the bishopric's question, and so now, there was only thing to do: solve the problem. My father and brother helped me construct a padded platform that would serve as the firm surface I needed. I selected clothes from my wardrobe that were loose fitting and would be the easiest to put on. Then I began to try to get dressed by myself, from socks and shoes to pants and shirt.

My seminary class was scheduled to begin at 6:15 every weekday morning. To be prepared and have the classroom set up for the lesson, I would need to leave my home before 5:30 A.M. I arose at 2:30 that first morning to attempt the task.

In my younger years, I had wrestled with a lot of things: my brother, bad habits, and with difficult decisions, but I had never once experienced wrestling with myself . . . especially not for two-and-a-half hours! Using every available resource I had — teeth, arms, hands with fingers that refused to work, and shoulders, I struggled to get dressed. By 5:30 I was physically exhausted, but I was dressed and ready for seminary. I had accomplished something that had seemed impossible, realized a dream, passed a significant milestone, and made it to a plateau many thought I could never reach.

During the weeks and months that followed I made significant progress. The task that had initially taken me two-and-a-half hours and required every ounce of strength I possessed, was reduced to less than twenty minutes. And for the next year-and-a-half I taught early-morning seminary. It was a dream that had come true.

I have learned that victory is assured when we acquire the willingness to do whatever it takes, and the resolve to never give up. Perhaps Sir Winston Churchill stated it best. He sought to strengthen the courage of the people of England when they were being threatened during World War II by Hitler, and by what seemed to be an invincible Nazi force. He declared: "We have before us an ordeal of the most grievous kind. We have before us many, many months of struggle and of suffering. You ask what is our policy? I will say: It is to wage war, by sea, land, and air, with all our might and with all our strength that God can give us . . . That is our policy. You ask what is our aim? I can answer in one word: Victory — victory at all costs, victory in spite of terror;

victory, however long and hard the road may be." ("Churchill: The Life Triumphant," *American Heritage,* 1965, p. 90.) Is it any wonder that they triumphed?

Art E. Berg is a businessman and president of Invictus Communications, Inc. A professional motivational speaker to church and youth groups, he is the author of a book entitled, Some Miracles Take Time. *His recreational interests are wheelchair racing, parasailing, boating, and traveling. Art enjoys working with youth and has served as a Sunday School teacher, Aaronic Priesthood adviser, and a seminary instructor. He is married to Dallas Howard Berg, and they are the parents of one child.*

3

IS IT LOVE OR JUST SOMETHING I ATE?

RANDALL BIRD

Quite a few years ago I came across a poem that I have just loved. The author is unknown, but I would like you to read it since it is the focus for the message I would like to deliver.

INDIAN LOVE POEM

Nice night
In June
Star shine
Big moon.
In park
On bench
With girl
In clinch.
Me say
"Me love"
She coo
Like dove.
Me smart
Me fast
Never let
Chance past.
"Get hitched,"
Me say
She say
"Okay."

Wedding bells
Ring . . . Ring
Honeymoon
Everything.
Settle down
Married life
Everything
Happy life.
'Nother night
In June
Stars shine
Big moon.
No happy
No more
Carry baby
Walk floor.
Wife mad
She fuss
Me mad
Me cuss.
Life one
Big spat
Naggy wife
Bawling brat.
Realize
At last —
Me too
Darn fast.

President David O. McKay, in his book *Gospel Ideals*, mentioned that he was once asked, "How may I know when I am in love?" His reply is so excellent.

That is a very important question. A fellow student and I considered that query one night as we walked together. As boys of that age frequently do, we were talking about girls. Neither he nor I knew whether or not we were in love. Of course I had not then met my present sweetheart. In answer to my question, "How may we know when we are in love?" he replied: "My mother once said that if you meet a girl in whose presence you feel a desire to achieve, who inspires you to do your best, and to make the most of yourself, such a young woman is worthy of your love and is awakening love in your heart."

I submit that as a true guide. In the presence of the girl you truly love you do not feel to grovel; in her presence you do not attempt to take advantage of her; in her presence you feel that you would like to be everything that a "Master Man" should become, for she will inspire you to that ideal. And I ask you young women to cherish that same guide. What does he inspire in you—to feel as Portia did when she loved? She was wealthy; she was beautiful; but for Bassanio she wished she were a thousand times more beautiful, ten thousand times richer—that is what true love does. When a young man accompanies you after a meeting, or after a dance, and he shows an inclination to use you as a convenience or as a means of gratification, then you may put it down that he is not prompted by love.

Under such circumstances, no matter how fascinated you may be, young woman, no matter how confident you may feel that you love him, let your judgment rule and be master of your feelings. It may grieve you not to follow the inclination of your heart, but you had better be pained a little in your youth than to suffer pangs of torture later. (David O. McKay, *Gospel Ideals* [Salt Lake City: The Improvement Era, 1953], pp. 459-60.)

What a beautiful message from a prophet. To follow this great counsel would be a blessing in all of our lives.

It should be noted that we do not simply arrive at the mature stage of love that President McKay and his beloved wife, Emma, achieved. Instead we go through various stages in life that prepare us for such an experience. Let's examine these stages of love together.

BABY STAGE

The first level of love we all go through, I'll call the "baby stage" of love. This stage is a totally dependent stage. It's best demonstrated by thinking of an infant who has to be fed, changed, burped, and everything by someone other than himself. The baby is not able to do those things on his own, and is totally dependent on someone else to provide his needs. I have already noted that this is a stage that we all go through. But can you imagine being *stuck* in the baby stage of love? If a married couple were mired in this kind of a relationship, the husband would come home from work and say to his wife and children, "Honey, bring me the paper. Kids, get me a pillow, and take off my shoes. I want some dinner. Change the channel."

Can you see how being stuck in this stage would not be a fun experience for a partner? That's right, the husband would basically be saying, "Feed me. Change me. Burp me."

POSSESSIVE STAGE

This stage is usually characterized by selfishness — a love of self and one's possessions. Two-year-old children demonstrate "possessive" behavior. You've probably observed toddlers at play. If they set a toy down to pursue some other adventure, but notice another child picking the toy up, they quickly come back to claim it. They have learned to say, "My toy. Leave it alone," and if they aren't able to get their way, they may scream or cry.

It's not uncommon for teenagers or even adults to be stuck in the possessive stage. Picture in your mind a young man speaking to his girlfriend in this manner: "Now, listen. You're my girlfriend! I don't want you talking to other people. If you do, well, let's just say, it's either me or them." Then, he may walk off and flirt with other girls, or even date them. But if someone else shows an interest in the girl he wants to possess, then he rushes back to his "toy" and tries to reclaim her. You've seen it, haven't you?

LOVE OF FRIENDS AND PARENTS

It's interesting to note that, as we mature, we find ourselves more willing to do for others. King Benjamin taught "that when ye are in the service of your fellow beings ye are only in the service of your God" (Mosiah 2:17). I've always enjoyed observing young children and youth as they discover how good it makes them feel to touch the lives of other people — as they learn to give instead of just receive. It is so much fun to watch what happens when a young child does the dishes without being asked. After the task is completed, the anonymous dishwasher waits anxiously for the deed to be discovered, and then bursts into a big smile when Mom finally identifies the "culprit."

It's also thrilling to see the youth of the Church become involved in service projects. They sometimes moan, complain, and occasionally murmur when the assignment is announced. But, what a sight when the service is completed! The faces of the participants very nearly glow with happiness.

I remember being in a southern state several years ago where a youth conference was being held. The theme of the conference was service. The young people were divided into teams and given a list of service projects they could perform for citizens in the community. Each project was assigned a certain number of points, with the most points being given for the placement of a copy of the Book of Mormon. The team that accumulated the most points would be the winner.

Youth traveled throughout the city asking people if they could perform acts of service. Some people were initially dubious, but when they became convinced there was no "catch," they invited the young people to wash windows, clean flower beds, rake leaves, wash dogs, and even change babies' diapers. It was exciting to see how good the youth felt as they performed and completed these tasks. The reward was far greater than if they had been paid money for the jobs. They experienced feelings of love and gratification that cannot be found in any other way. Everyone involved was grateful for the chance to participate.

INFATUATION

Since we have four daughters, our home often felt like a girl's dormitory. I enjoyed listening to the conversations our girls would have with their mother after school. The topic was frequently boys, and it always seemed like a life-or-death situation. One would nearly swoon as she told how she got to sit next to the best-looking guy in seminary, while another would anguish as she tried to imagine how a certain boy could possibly like some other girl.

One of the things I enjoyed doing in high school was sitting in the opposing team's cheering section during games, and listening to the kids from the other school evaluate the boys and girls from our school. You would hear comments like, "Oh, kid, what a babe!" or "Why doesn't our school have boys that look like that?" There were obviously a lot of fantasies being created.

Generally speaking, girls mature earlier than boys. The result is that girls will gather into groups and make comments like, "The boys our age are *so* immature. What we need is to find some men who will *appreciate* us." This social phenomenon usually begins to take place about the junior high years. It's not uncommon for a junior high school girl to be walking down the street, and have a high school boy drive by in his car and wave to her. She is so excited. She can't wait to get with her group of girls so that she can share this romantic experience.

That's another thing. Have you noticed how often girls seem to be in groups? At a dance a boy nearly always has to plow through the group to ask a girl to dance. And I remember one time a girl in a class I was teaching raised her hand to ask permission to go to the rest room. When she stood up to leave, three or four other girls insisted they had to go with her.

Anyway, the girl who has been waved at hurries to her group. She squeals, "You guys. Guess who just waved to me?"

"Who?"

"Jack!"

"Jack, the quarterback?"

"Yes!"

"Well, how did he wave?"

The first girl approximates the gesture Jack made as he drove by, and the girls all scream in unison, their faces as flushed as if they had just won a million dollars.

Infatuation is purely a physical thing. Don't let it get out of hand. Elder Marvin J. Ashton, of the Quorum of the Twelve, has said:

> True love is a process. True love requires personal action. Love must be continuing to be real. Love takes time. Too often

expediency, infatuation, stimulation, persuasion, or lust are mistaken for love. How hollow, how empty if our love is no deeper than the arousal of momentary feeling or the expression in words of what is no more lasting than the time it takes to speak them. (*What Is Your Destination?* [Salt Lake City: Deseret Book, 1978], p. 51.)

Wouldn't it be sad to be married to a partner who lived totally for the physical side of life? That kind of person would constantly compare you with those they felt were more beautiful or handsome. You certainly would not be a "happy camper" in that situation.

ROMANTIC LOVE

Mature love is based less on physical attraction than on spiritual attraction. The greater capacity we have to love Heavenly Father and the Savior, the greater capacity we will have to love our marriage partner. By *romantic*, I certainly don't mean what the movies, television, and most literature portray as romantic. Once when I visited with a group of high school seniors and young adults, the girls informed me that what they really want in a relationship is not so much physical intimacy as kindness, demonstrated with words, conversation, and gestures of respect. They do not, they said, enjoy being treated like some object. This is in keeping with what the Lord has told us through his prophets — that we be willing to do everything within our power to protect the virtue of those with whom we associate. In his Sermon on the Mount, the Savior himself said, "Therefore all things whatsoever ye would that men should do to you, do ye even so to them" (Matthew 7:12).

Maybe an analogy will help. Imagine your little brother or sister standing in the middle of the road, and that he or she is unaware of the approach of a speeding truck. Rather than witness the death of a little child that you love, you would likely sacrifice your own life, if necessary, to knock them out of harm's way. We ought to feel no less dedicated to safeguarding the virtue of those we date.

MATURE LOVE

In an article entitled, "Be My Valentine, Pass It On," Bill Alder collected messages sent by young children to one another on Valentine's Day. Consider some of these unpredictable, warm, wild, and romantic valentines.

Dear Robert,
I think I am in love with you, but I will have to ask my mother before I can be sure.
Love,
Celeste

Dear Joseph,
You are the dumbest, ugliest boy I ever met, but I love you because nobody is perfect.
Love,
Angela

Dear Robert,
I think you are the handsomest boy in the class.
Love,
Susie
P.S. Who do you think is the prettiest?

Even though these letters reflect a childlike love, it's the beginning of the very love that leads us toward that perfect love that Christ would have us possess.

I found a list in my files that defines ten characteristics of mature love. I do not know who wrote them, but they are wonderful.

Ten Tests of Mature Love

1. Love is outgoing.
    a. It is centered in the other person's well-being and welfare.
    b. If he/she is happy, then you are, and vice versa.
    c. Put the other person first.
2. Real love releases energy.

    a. You would lay the world at her/his feet.

    b. Want to live up to her/his expectations.

3. Love wants to share.

    a. Share each discovery or thrill of life.

4. You must like as well as love.

    a. You are proud of this person.

    b. You can't reform, you need to respect.

5. Love is a "we" feeling.

    a. You talk of and do things as a team.

6. Time is the surest test.

    a. Real love will endure, don't be in a hurry.

    b. Test it under all circumstances of real life.

7. Would this person make an excellent father or mother to your children?

    a. See how they treat younger members of the family.

    b. Watch how they speak and act toward parents.

8. Your love is spiritual — not just physical.

    a. You can share spiritual experiences together.

    b. You can pray, read scriptures, and do other spiritual things together.

9. This person is a genuine companion to you.

    a. You can talk things over easily.

    b. Play and do things together.

10. You meet on common ground mentally, socially, and spiritually.

    a. You share fundamental goals, aims, and standards of life.

    b. Are you interested in some of the same things?

I hope that we understand that a true or mature love is tender, unselfish, cooperative, and growing. It is built upon high ideals, and strengthened by shared experiences and trials.

President Spencer W. Kimball summarized true love by saying:

> It is a total partnership. It is companionship with common ideals and standards. It is unselfishness toward and sacrifice for one another. . . . This kind of love never tires or wanes. It lives on through sickness and sorrow, through prosperity and privation, through accomplishment and disappointment, through

time and eternity. . . . It will be a far greater and more intensified love, grown quieter and more dignified with the years of sacrifice, suffering, joys, and consecration to one another, to your family, and to the kingdom of God. [Author: Source?]

May we continue to progress towards the true charity that would make us, and those we associate with, more God-like. I pray this, humbly, in the name of Jesus Christ, Amen.

Randall C. Bird has taught seminary for more than twenty years and is currently employed by the Church Education System as a teacher trainer. Brother Bird has had a life-long interest in athletics and during his high school years was named to the Idaho all-state teams in football and track. He has since been a high school coach in both sports. He enjoys fishing, collecting sports memorabilia, and reading. He and his wife, Carla, have six children.

4

WHY ARE THERE SO MANY CHURCHES?

JOHN BYTHEWAY

Would you believe your testimony could double after reading this chapter? That's what happened to me when I began to read and gather information instead of wasting time watching TV. I wanted to know why there are so many churches, and where they all came from, and why we say we are the only true church. I was led on an interesting, surprising, and sometimes depressing journey through history. Get your scriptures, and accompany me as we explore the New Testament church, the Great Apostasy, the Dark Ages, the Reformation, and the Restoration.

30 A.D. — 325 A.D.

As you know, in about 30 A.D., Jesus was crucified. Three days later, he was resurrected. He stayed with the apostles for a time and then ascended to heaven. Because of Judas's suicide, there were only eleven apostles. The remaining apostles met to fill the vacancy: "And they prayed, and said, Thou, Lord, which knowest the hearts of all men, shew whether of these two thou hast chosen, that he may take part of this ministry and apostleship, from which Judas by transgression fell, that he might go to his own place. And they gave forth their lots; and the lot fell upon Matthias; and he was numbered with the eleven apostles" (Acts 1:24–26).

Clearly, it was the intention of the Lord that the Quorum of the Twelve should continue. Notice also that the apostles did not take it upon themselves to choose a new successor, but they prayed for inspiration, ensuring that the new member would be called of God, as they had been (see John 15:16 and Hebrews 5:4).

In Old Testament times, prophets foresaw the day when the true gospel would not be on the earth. There would be a "falling away," or an apostasy. "Behold, the days come, saith the Lord God, that I will send a famine in the land, not a famine of bread, nor a thirst for water, but of hearing the words of the Lord: and they shall wander from sea to sea, and from the north even to the east, they shall run to and fro to seek the word of the Lord, and shall not find it" (Amos 8:11–12).[1]

God knew that this apostasy would take place, and had prepared for the gospel to be restored. Peter prophesied of this when he told the Jews: "He shall send Jesus Christ, . . . whom the heaven must receive until the times of *restitution of all things,* which God hath spoken by the mouth of all his holy prophets since the world began" (Acts 3:20–21; emphasis added).

Restitution means restoration (of course, something must be lost before it can be restored). Many believed the second coming of Jesus Christ would take place very soon after his ascension. Paul wrote to those who were mistaken on this point: "Be not soon shaken in mind, or be troubled, neither by spirit, nor by word, nor by letter as from us, as that the day of Christ is at hand. Let no man deceive you by any means: for that day shall not come, except there come a falling away first" (2 Thessalonians 2:2–3; emphasis added).

After Jesus was resurrected, he charged the apostles, "Go ye into all the world, and preach the gospel to every creature" (Mark 16:15). This the apostles did, and, except for John, they were all eventually killed. John Foxe's *Book of Martyrs* accounts for the death of the apostles as follows: Peter was crucified at Rome, head downward. James (the son of Zebedee) was beheaded. John was banished to the Isle of Patmos. Bartholomew was beaten, crucified, and then beheaded. James (the son of Alphaeus) was stoned and beaten to death. Matthew was slain with a halberd. Andrew, Simon (Zelotes), Thaddeus, and Philip were crucified.

Thomas was killed with a spear. Matthias was stoned and then beheaded. Paul was beheaded in Rome by Nero.[2]

John was taken out of the ministry, and nothing is heard of him after about 101 A.D. Elder Mark E. Petersen explains that John was not permitted to tarry longer in Patmos because wickedness had nearly taken over the church. Doctrines and ordinances were changed, authority was ignored, and sin became rampant, even among the membership of the church.[3]

The apostles were unable to meet and fill the vacancies in the twelve, as they had done before. Bishops (*local* authorities) of the many cities were left without the priesthood supervision of the apostles (*general* authorities). False teachers and false doctrines arose. This is confirmed in the writings of Eusebius, an ancient historian who lived about 260–339 A.D.

> "The Church continued until then [the close of the 1st Century] as a pure and uncorrupt virgin, whilst if there were any at all that attempted to pervert the sound doctrine of the saving gospel, they were yet skulking in dark retreats: but *when the sacred choir of Apostles became extinct* and the generation of those that had been privileged to hear their inspired wisdom had passed away, then also the *combinations of impious errors arose* by the fraud and delusions of false teachers. These also as there were none of the apostles left, henceforth attempted without shame, to preach their *false doctrines against the gospel truth*"[4] (emphasis added).

A modern historian(non-LDS) agrees with Eusebius that the death of the apostles marked the beginning of the apostasy: "With the close of the New Testament records, and the death of the last surviving apostle, the history of the church passes from its sacred to its purely human phase. The miraculous gifts which attested the Divine mission of the apostles ceased; not indeed by any formal record of their withdrawal, but by the *clear evidence that they were possessed no longer* (emphasis added).[5]

During the next two centuries, the church drifted without direction. Horrible, government-sponsored persecutions were inflicted on the Christians, and they were forced underground. The pure doctrines of the gospel were corrupted by the prevailing pagan religions and the philosophies of men. Disagreements arose on many doctrines, including the mode of baptism and the nature of God.

In the mid-third century, a man named Cyprian, who was the Bishop of Carthage, advocated the use of sprinkling instead of immersion when the candidate for baptism had some physical weakness.[6] This method caught on, and became widespread. A few centuries later, the practice of baptizing infants began.[7]

325 A.D. — 1045 A.D.

Persecutions continued, but Christianity would not go away. The emperor of Rome, Constantine, saw the possibility of gaining personal political advantage by supporting Christianity. He thought it might strengthen his empire to endorse Christianity and make it the state religion. Constantine assembled a council of all Bishops in 325 A.D., to settle a dispute concerning the nature of God. Some argued that the Father and the Son were of the same substance, and others that they were distinct individuals. The council concluded its debates by issuing the Nicean "Creed," or statement of belief. By vote and some coercion by Constantine, the doctrine of the Trinity emerged, basically a product of debate and compromise. There was no revelation, no authority, no attempt at inspiration. The formation of this council was also the first step in making the church a department of the Roman Empire.

Thus we can see that in only a few centuries after Christ, the apostasy was essentially complete. Priesthood leadership and authority was lost, the nature of God was changed by vote, the mode of baptism was altered, and Constantine, an uninspired, unbaptized sun-worshiper who committed murder within his own family, was appointing new Bishops.[8] Constantine's plan to unite the empire under one religion was successful, and this new church would eventually be called the "universal" or "Catholic" church.

This was essentially the only Christian church in existence for several centuries, its history characterized by power struggles, intrigue, and heresy. A historian (non-LDS) describing these years said: "It seemed impossible that things could become worse; yet Rome had still to see Benedict IX, A.D. 1033, a boy of less than twelve years, raised to the apostolic throne. Of this pontiff, one of his successors, Victor III, declared that his life was so shameful, so foul, so execrable, that he shuddered to describe it. He ruled like a captain of banditti rather than a prelate. The people at last, unable to bear his adulteries, homicides and abominations any longer, rose up against him. In despair of maintaining his position, he put up the papacy to auction. It was bought by a presbyter named John, who became Gregory VI, A.D. 1045."[8]

1045 A.D. – 1440 A.D.

The church had changed from a persecut*ed* church to a persecut*ing* church. More basic doctrines were altered. Instead of a worship service where the membership participated, the mass became more of a performance with much pomp, mystery, and ceremony. Then in 1054, long-standing rivalries over where the seat of church government should be located resulted in a splitting of the church into the Roman Catholic Church, with headquarters in Rome, and the Greek Orthodox Church, with headquarters in Constantinople, Greece.

The western church developed faster than the eastern church. The Roman church filled Europe but was ruled from Rome. Those who disagreed with the doctrines or practices of the church were called heretics and were usually tortured and killed. Not surprisingly, the many centuries when there was no priesthood and no revelation on the earth are referred to by almost all historians as the "Dark Ages." The "Light of the world" had been extinguished.

During this time very few copies of the Bible were in existence. They had to be hand copied and were very expensive. The church actually discouraged reading the scriptures, reserving that right for the clergy only. This condition persisted until 1440, when the printing press came into existence. Its use eventually made copies of the Bible more widely available. You would think that this advance would have been welcomed by the church, but interestingly enough, the church was violently opposed to the development of printing. Elder Bruce R. McConkie observed: "Few tools were more effective than printing in paving the way for the great revival of learning, for the religious reformation, and for the breaking away of peoples and nations from religious domination. Without the discovery of movable type in about 1440 A.D. the barrier of gross darkness covering the apostate world could scarce have been pierced. One of the first books published was the Gutenberg Bible in 1456 A.D.

"Perhaps no important discovery in world history ever faced such intense and bitter opposition as arose over the use and spread of printing. Civil and ecclesiastical tyrants feared the loss of their ill-held and evilly-exercised powers should knowledge and truth be made available to people generally. 'We must root out printing,' said the Vicar of Croydon from his pulpit, 'or printing will root us out.' "[10]

1440 A.D. – 1830 A.D.

Despite the opposition, printing flourished, and the scriptures were read by ever-increasing numbers of people. There was at this time a concurrent great revival of learning and of the arts. This period marks the end of the Dark Ages, and is often called the renaissance.

Now we begin to see the hand of the Lord preparing the "restitution of all things" spoken of by Peter. In 1492, Christopher Columbus set off to find a shorter route to India, an event foreseen by ancient prophets (see 1 Nephi 13:12).

With time, more and more people came to study the scriptures. A monk and university professor named Martin Luther became concerned about certain abuses and practices of the church. In 1517, he prepared a list of 95 theses (subjects for debate), and nailed them to the door of the All Saints Church in Wittenberg, Germany.

The Catholic church did not appreciate Luther's dissension, and eventually he was forced into hiding. Luther had friends in high places or else he probably would have been killed, as were many others who protested practices in the church. While in hiding, Luther continued to write. Some agreed with Luther; others opposed him. King Henry VIII of England published a book in defense of the church, for which he was awarded the title "Defender of the Faith," a title that is still carried by British monarchs. Luther gained a following and his movement eventually resulted in the formation of a "new" church called the Lutheran Church. Martin Luther is recognized as the first "protestant," and his movement marks the beginning of the "Reformation." Actually, it was not Luther's original intent to form a new church. He said, "I have sought nothing beyond reforming the Church in conformity with the Holy Scriptures. The spiritual powers have been not only corrupted by sin, but absolutely destroyed; so that there is now nothing in them but a depraved reason and a will that is the enemy and opponent of God. I simply say that Christianity has ceased to exist among those who should have preserved it."[11]

Tension had been mounting for some time between the Church in Rome and the governments of some European nations. A portion of the taxes collected by these governments was sent to Rome. Tensions reached a peak in England when in 1529, Henry VIII desired a divorce from his wife, Catherine of Aragon. The pope would not grant this divorce, and in 1535 parliament declared Henry VIII the supreme head of the church in England. Thus, Henry VIII became head of both church and state in England, giving him the authority to grant his own divorce. Some in the church in England refused to recognize this action, and Henry had many of them executed. Ties with the Roman church were formally broken, and the Church of England, also called the Anglican, and in America, the Episcopalian Church, was born.

Another group, observing from the Bible that baptism was performed only on those capable of repenting, was eventually formed into a church by John Smyth in 1609. This group performed baptisms first by pouring and later by immersion. Others referred to them as "Anabaptists" or rebaptizers. Persecutions raged against them, and many Anabaptists were publicly drowned. The Anabaptists were the beginning of the Baptist movement.

It was only eleven years later, in 1620, that the passengers on the *Mayflower* set sail for America in search of religious freedom. Seven ancestors of Joseph Smith were on board.

In 1639, in Providence, Rhode Island, a puritan minister named Roger Williams founded the first Baptist church in America. In this remarkable statement, Williams declared his belief that a *reformation* was not enough — a *restoration* was needed."There is no regularly constituted church on earth, nor any person qualified to administer any church ordinances; nor can there be until *new apostles are sent* by the Great Head of the Church for whose coming I am seeking"(emphasis added).[12]

John Calvin and John Knox were the forces behind the protestant movement called Presbyterianism, which was formed about 1649. The word *Presbyterian* refers to a representative form of church government. In Greek, *presbyteros* means elder.[13] Calvin and Knox formed a church government similar in form to that of the Christian church in the first century. This is how the Presbyterian church came into existence.

John and Charles Wesley were brothers who attended Oxford University in England. They formed the "Holy Club," and were nicknamed "methodists" by the student body because of their strict and methodical rules of conduct and religious observance. John Wesley did not intend to organize a new sect, but gained many followers when he began to preach in about 1738. The first Methodist church in America was formally established in 1784.[14] How did John Wesley feel about traditional Christianity? "It does not appear that these extraordinary gifts of the Holy Ghost were common in the Church for more than two or three centuries. We seldom hear of them after that fatal period when the Emperor Constantine called himself a Christian. . . . From this time they almost totally ceased. . . . The Christians had no more of the Spirit of Christ than the other heathens. . . . This was the real cause why the extraordinary gifts of the Holy Ghost were no longer to be found in the Christian Church; because the Christians were turned heathen again, and had only a dead form left."[15]

In 1776 the Declaration of Independence was signed, and in 1791 the Bill of Rights, which guaranteed religious freedom, was finally ratified. One of the signers of the declaration, and one of our founding fathers, was Thomas Jefferson. Read what Jefferson had to say, and ask yourself if he was inspired: "The religion builders have so distorted and deformed the doctrines of Jesus, so muffled them in mysticisms, fancies and falsehoods, have caricatured them into forms so inconceivable, as to shock reasonable thinkers. . . . *Happy in the prospect of a restoration of primitive Christianity,* I must leave to younger persons to encounter and lop off the false branches which have been engrafted into it by the mythologists of the middle and modern ages" (emphasis added).[16]

Only fourteen years later, Joseph Smith was born in Sharon, Vermont. There is not room to retell his story here. I hope you will stop here and read it for yourself in Joseph Smith—History in the Pearl of Great Price.

In short, young Joseph, confused by the many religionists who argued and contended one with another, went to pray. His question was *not* "is there a true church?" Apparently, he thought one of them might be true. His question was "which one should I join?" In response to Joseph's prayer, the heavens were opened, and Father in Heaven once again spoke to his children on the earth. The true nature of God was revealed; the priesthood restored, with the authority to baptize; and a "voice from the dust," the Book of Mormon, containing the "everlasting gospel," was brought forth (see Revelation 14:6). All things that had been altered or lost were restored.

WHY ARE THERE SO MANY CHURCHES, AND WHERE DID THEY ALL COME FROM?

Originally, there was only the church of Jesus Christ. But, as prophesied, the church was taken from the earth. People were left to interpret the scriptures without the aid of a prophet. The philosophies of men corrupted the pure doctrines of Christ, the church fell into apostasy, and the Dark Ages ensued. At the close of the Dark Ages, "the spirit of inspiration rested upon the reformers, causing them to rebel against the religious evils of the day and seek to make the Bible and other truth available to all who would receive such."[17] The reformation resulted in many different churches all trying to return to the pure doctrine of Christ. However, none of them had the proper authority, and most of them retained ideas and philosophies from the Roman church that had been corrupted centuries earlier.

WHY DO WE SAY WE ARE THE ONLY TRUE CHURCH?

Because Jesus Christ said so. In the revelation that became the preface to the Doctrine and Covenants, the Lord acknowledged the Church as "the only true and living church upon the face of the whole earth" (Doctrine and Covenants 1:30). Take note, it is not only the *true* church, it is a *living* church. It is living because he lives, and he is the head of it. Under his guidance and direction, his church was reestablished on the earth. A reformation wasn't enough. A restoration was needed.

We make a lot of enemies with our contention that we belong to the only true church, and we need to be careful. We must always recognize that there are many wonderful people who are honest in heart who are members of other churches, or not members of any church at all. It is one of the tenets of our belief to be tolerant of all religions. "We claim the privilege of worshiping Almighty God according to the dictates of our own conscience, and allow all men the same privilege, let them worship how, where, or what they may" (11th Article of Faith).

Coupled with this belief is the charge given to the original apostles that has been given again in our day: "Go ye into all the world, preach the gospel to every creature, acting in the authority which I have given you, baptizing in the name of the Father, and of the Son, and of the Holy Ghost" (Doctrine and Covenants 68:8).

How do others react to our claim of being the only true church? Some of the responses are quite interesting. Orson F. Whitney relates this experience:

> Many years ago a learned man, a member of the Roman Catholic Church, came to Utah and spoke from the stand of the Salt Lake Tabernacle. I became well-acquainted with him, and

we conversed freely and frankly. A great scholar, with perhaps a dozen languages at his tongue's end, he seemed to know all about theology, law, literature, science and philosophy. One day he said to me: "You Mormons are all ignoramuses. You don't even know the strength of your own position. It is so strong that there is only one other tenable in the whole Christian World, and that is the position of the Catholic Church. The issue is between Catholicism and Mormonism. If we are right, you are wrong; if you are right, we are wrong; and that's all there is to it. The Protestants haven't a leg to stand on. For, if we are wrong, they are wrong with us, since they were a part of us and went out from us; while if we are right, they are apostates whom we cut off long ago. If we have the apostolic succession from St. Peter, as we claim, there is no need of Joseph Smith and Mormonism; but if we have not that succession, then such a man as Joseph Smith was necessary, and Mormonism's attitude is the only consistent one. It is either the perpetuation of the gospel from ancient times, or the restoration of the gospel in latter days."[18]

From what we have already seen, many of the Reformers were convinced of the apostasy, at least to some degree. How would they respond to the message of the restoration? How would the Founding Fathers respond? Wilford Woodruff reports:

I will say here, before closing, that two weeks before I left St. George, the spirits of the dead gathered around me, wanting to know why we did not redeem them. Said they: "You have had the use of the Endowment House for a number of years and yet nothing has ever been done for us. We laid the foundation of the government you now enjoy, and we never apostatized from it, but we remained true to it and were faithful to God." These were the signers of the Declaration of Independence, and they waited on me for two days and two nights. I thought it very singular that notwithstanding so much work had been done, and yet nothing had been done for them. The thought never entered my heart from the fact, I suppose, that heretofore our minds were reaching after our more immediate friends and relatives. I straightway went into the baptismal font and called upon Brother McAllister to baptize me for the signers of the Declaration of Independence, and fifty other eminent men, making one hundred in all, including John Wesley, Columbus, and others; I then baptized him for every president of the United States except three; and when their cause is just, somebody will do the work for them.[19]

At times I have pondered about living in the days of Jesus. I've wondered if I would have been open-minded enough to believe in him, or if I would have been skeptical like the scribes and Pharisees. I find great comfort in this statement of Bruce R. McConkie:

> Who will honor the name of Joseph Smith and accept the gospel restored through his instrumentality? We answer: The same people who would have believed the words of the Lord Jesus and the ancient Apostles and prophets had they lived in their day.
>
> If you believe the words of Joseph Smith, you would have believed what Jesus and the ancients said. If you reject Joseph Smith and his message, you would have rejected Peter and Paul and their message.[20]

My "academic" testimony continues to grow as I study the events of the apostasy and the restoration. An academic testimony is something you believe because it makes sense — because it's logical. Now you can pray about these things and gain a spiritual testimony. And here's the exciting part — the more you learn (academically), the more the Spirit can confirm to your heart (spiritually).

I give my witness of the restoration. The gospel is true. The Holy Ghost testifies of it, and so does history. We are privileged to be here during this time. We also have a great responsibility. President Ezra Taft Benson said this of you and your generation:

> For nearly six thousand years, God has held you in reserve to make your appearance in the final days before the second coming. Every previous gospel dispensation has drifted into apostasy, but ours will not. God has saved for the final inning, some of his strongest children, who will help bear off the kingdom triumphant, and that is where you come in. For you are the generation that must be prepared to meet your God.[21]

I hope this chapter has helped to answer some of your questions. The scriptures tell us to "obtain a knowledge of history, and of countries, and of kingdoms, of laws of God and man, and all this for the salvation of Zion" (Doctrine & Covenants 93:53). Knowledge is power, and there is so much to learn! You are part of the restoration of the gospel. I challenge you to turn off the TV, get into "the best books" (see Doctrine & Covenants 88:79, 118; 90:15), especially the scriptures and the writings of the living prophets, and fortify your spirit for the final days before the Second Coming.

1. See also Isa. 24:1–6; Matt. 24:9–12; Acts 20:29–30; 1 Tim. 4:1–3; 2 Tim. 3:1–5; 2 Peter 2:1–3; 1 Nephi 13:24–29, Topical Guide; "Apostasy of the Early Christian Church."

2. John Foxe, *Book of Martyrs*, Book I, pp. 27–32.

3. Mark E. Petersen, *Which Church Is Right?*, 1974.

4. Eusebius Ecclesiastical History, Book III, Chapter 32 (Eusebius is quoting Hegesippus).

5. Dr. Phillip Smith, *Students Ecclesiastical History*, vol. I, p. 62., emphasis added.

6. Eusebius, *History of the Church*, Book VI, chapter 43.

7. James E. Talmage, *The Great Apostasy*, pp. 118–19. See also B. H. Roberts, *Outlines of Ecclesiastical History*, p. 141; Eusebius, *History of the Church*, Book VI, Chapter 43.

8. Mark E. Petersen, *Which Church Is Right?* p. 12.

9. John William Draper, *Intellectual Development of Europe*, volume I, pp. 378–382., as cited in *The Falling Away*, B. H. Roberts, p. 125. See also *A History of the Popes*, Sir Nicolas Cheetham, 1982, Dorset Press.)

10. *Progress of Man*, pp. 206–215., Bruce R. McConkie, *Mormon Doctrine* p. 716.

11. In Galat. (1535) Weins IX, P.I. 293, 24–27, p. 50, Luther and His Times, p. 509, Martin Luther p. 188.

12. *Picturesque America*, p. 502, emphasis added.

13. *Religions of America*, edited by Leo Rosten, pp. 200–01.

14. *Religions of America*, edited by Leo Rosten, pp. 172–73.

15. Wesley's Works, vol. 7, Sermon 89, pp. 26–27.

16. Jefferson's Complete Works, vol. 7, pp. 210 and 257., emphasis added.

17. Bruce R. McConkie, *Mormon Doctrine*, p. 717.

18. LeGrand Richards, *A Marvelous Work and a Wonder*, p. 3.

19. Wilford Woodruff, General Conference, September 16, 1877, also *Journal of Discourses*, Vol. 19, p. 229.

20. Bruce R. McConkie, *Ensign*, November 1981, p. 48.

21. Ezra Taft Benson, cited by Marvin J. Ashton, *Ensign*, November 1989, p. 36.

John G. Bytheway, an administrator in Continuing Education at Brigham Young University, is currently working on a master's degree in Instructional Science. A popular speaker with an interest in youthful members of the Church, Brother Bytheway is a frequent participant at Education Week and Especially for Youth sessions. He has an interest in cars and aviation and enjoys reading, running, and playing the guitar.

BIRDS OF A FEATHER

VIVIAN CLINE

Have you ever thought about the importance of clothing in our lives? Sure, we know that clothes cover our nakedness, but they do far more than that. The fact is, the clothing we wear reveals a great deal about us. It tends to give us identity and tells others what is important to us and how we want to be treated. It can also be an indication of our pride and values. Additionally, it can actually influence how we feel about ourselves, and determine what our mood will be.

Some examples of how our clothing indicates who we are and how we want to be treated can be seen around your own school.

Think for a moment about the different "groups" you see at your school and what makes them distinctive. One easy way to identify members of these groups is by the clothing they tend to wear.

Some schools have groups called "preppies." Young people in this group wear conservative styles of clothing such as "Dockers," rugby shirts, golf shirts, and pullover sweaters. The guys often wear basic cotton oxford shirts, while the girls favor classic slacks, sweaters, skirts, and blouses. Specific labels and name brands are important to these people, and it is evident that wearing "the right clothes" is part of being included in the group.

Skaters are another group. They usually wear baggy shirts and pants, unlaced high-top tennis shoes, and sometimes wear their hair short in the back and long in the front so it can be worn to partially cover the eyes.

Cowboy groups are often found in western schools. Members are easily identified by their jeans, cowboy boots, and a leather belt with their name embossed on the back and a large shiny buckle on the front. Sometimes members of this group even wear cowboy hats.

Another group is the "rockers." These young people like to wear black, particularly if it has an image of their favorite rock group on it. From shirt to shoes they have no problem with color coordination. Sometimes they even die their hair black to match their clothes.

These are but a few examples. You can probably think of many more. The point, however, is very clear. Each person in the group wears the clothing that identifies him or her with others in that particular group.

Have you noticed that in nature, birds of the same species congregate in flocks? Bluebirds fly with bluebirds, and robins fly with robins. That is why we say, "Birds of a feather, flock together."

Like birds, people have a tendency to enjoy the company of people who share similar tastes, desires, ambitions, and preferences. Frequently, particularly in our youth, one of the ways people of similar mind-sets identify each other is by the way they dress — they wear the same "feathers," so to speak.

In this connection, how often do you see rockers hanging out with cowboys at school? Or how about preppies with skaters? Though they may speak to each other and casually interrelate, they don't usually choose to do things with each other or be best friends.

Have you ever wanted to change your feathers? Has the look of another group ever tempted you? Or have you ever used the way people were dressed to determine whether or not you wanted to sit by them or get to know them better?

When I went to high school, I suppose you could say I fit into the "preppie" group. I wore very conservative skirts and pants and plain penny-loafer shoes. Sweaters were the norm, and monograms were the hot thing. Everything you wore had to have your initials on it.

Some of my friends, however, began to dress like another group of that era. Members of this other group were called hippies.

Hippies wore bell-bottomed jeans, flowered shirts, and "love beads." If you have seen reruns of the old television show the "Brady Bunch," then you have a pretty good idea of that fashion statement.

As I watched some of my friends change their feathers (and their life-style), I became attracted to that look. I thought, "What harm could come from having one hippie outfit?" So off I went to buy a cool new set of feathers.

The outfit I bought was absolutely the coolest. The pants were tight fitting from the hip-hugger waist clear down to the knees, and then they suddenly flared from the knee to the ankle in one huge bell-bottom. They were navy blue in color and had a white vertical stripe about every three inches. I found a perfect shirt to match. It was solid navy blue and had lamb chop sleeves, tight cuffs with a million buttons, and a pointed collar that extended from my neck, half way down my chest. A leather and metal necklace, and a pair of moccasins, completed my perfectly hot new hippie outfit. Now I was dying to debut my new look.

At that time I was dating a very conservative young college man who was also a preppie. I decided to try out my new outfit when I went on my next date with him.

I'll never forget the look on my date's face when I opened the front door. His mouth dropped as he looked at my necklace, then my shirt, then my pants and moccasins, and back up to the shirt and necklace.

I could see his surprise, but I was eager to know his opinion of my new look.

I asked, "Well, what do you think?"

He bluntly said, "I think you look like a doggone hippie. Hurry and change your clothes before we are late for the show."

What would you have done? Would you have protested and said that if he didn't like you the way you were, he could take a hike?

Though my friend was not very tactful, I knew what he was trying to say. He had planned to go out with a bluebird, not a blackbird. He was taken back by my appearance, because I didn't look like what I really was. And though he knew what kind of bird I was inside, he preferred the familiar feathers that I normally wore. Then, too, he might have feared my becoming something else.

That is why what we wear is so significant. By continuing to wear that kind of clothing, I would have made my conservative friend uncomfortable around me. In time, those who were choosing to dress in that fashion might have taken me under their wing. In my youth that would have been unwise, because those who identified with the hippie movement were those who began experimenting with smoking pot and doing drugs. By dressing like them, I would have been identified by some people as one who did drugs too.

You see, people make assumptions about us based on the way we look and act. If we wear immodest clothing, chances are that people will assume that we are immodest. They will treat us accordingly, even though they may be mistaken about us.

We women are sometimes guilty of being immodest without even realizing it. We will see a new fashion look that might be a little brief, but really cute otherwise. We want to be in fashion so we buy and wear it. It might not even dawn on us that it is immodest until someone makes a comment or, worse, an advance. Only then do we realize that it is inappropriate for the kind of person we are and the sort of image that we want to project.

Another thing that clothing can do for us is to make us totally cool. Or can it?

In the bird species, some birds have strikingly bright or unusual feathers. With great pride they will strut around and flash their feathers to impress other birds. After all, their feathers are the coolest, and they have to let the other birds know it. Don't we humans sometimes do the same thing?

What would you think if I were to tell you that I had something that would make you the envy of all your friends? If you wore this thing, everyone would think you were the strongest, bravest, and most gorgeous person around. That without a doubt you would be the ultimate in cool. Everyone you met would want to be your friend. Would you be interested?

Okay. I'm going to give it to you. It's a smiley face the size of a half dollar, and I'm going to put it on the pocket of your shirt.

Well, how do you feel? Totally cool, right? No, you say! Oh, I'm sorry. I forgot one very important thing. I forgot to charge you $60.00 for the smiley face. Now you feel cool, right, because it cost so much?

By now you are probably saying to yourself, "This lady is really crazy."

As absurd as this example is, in reality we allow this to happen to us all the time.

Manufacturers take a simple article of clothing such as jeans, sew a triangle on the hip or a flag on the zipper, charge us an extra $60, and tell us that because of this label we are now totally cool. Believing them, we wear these feathers with great pride, displaying to others our advantage in cool.

Having been a clothing and textile major in college, I can tell you that some articles of clothing are better made than others. The weave of the fabric is better and the construction of the garment is better. However, denim is denim, and there is very little difference in the weight and quality of the material, regardless of the label sewn on it.

I don't know about you, but it infuriates me for the manufacturers to think they can manipulate me like that. They must think that my self-esteem is so low I need to pay them an exorbitant amount of money for a piece of clothing with a certain tag or label on it in order to be cool and accepted.

Do they really think that we are that dumb? Or are we? We aren't that vain and proud. Or are we? Are we allowing Satan to control us with our pride? Are our pride and vanity determining our values?

Jacob, the younger brother of Nephi, warned us about taking pride in material things. "And the hand of providence hath smiled upon you most pleasingly, that you have obtained many riches; and because some of you have obtained more abundantly than that of your brethren ye are lifted up in the pride of your hearts, and wear stiff necks and high heads because of the costliness of your apparel, and persecute your brethren because ye suppose that ye are better than they. And now, my brethren, do you suppose that God justifieth you in this thing? Behold, I say unto you, Nay. But he condemneth you, and if ye persist in these things his judgments must speedily come unto you" (Jacob 2:13–14).

Pride is such a strange thing. It sometimes slips up on us so gradually that we don't even recognize it.

Several years ago my husband and I were on a business trip out of state. After the meetings were over, we decided to go shopping at a local mall. Doug bought me a lovely outfit, and I was pleased. I told him what I really wanted, however, was a "teenaged" style outfit that would help me fit in more closely with the young girls.

We went into the junior department of this store, and Doug picked up a pair of slacks that were totally unique. They were a combination of black and dark green colors. Though I wasn't very impressed with the color, I matched a white blouse with a green stripe in it, and tried the outfit on.

When I came out of the fitting room, Doug's eyes lit up. "Wow," he said. "You look like a million bucks!" He paused, then said, "But, honey, you forgot to zip up your slacks all the way. Part of your shirt tail is hanging out of your zipper."

I quickly looked, and then I began laughing.

"That's not my shirt tail, silly," I said. "That is the brand name of the pants sewn to the zipper."

"Well, it looks stupid," Doug retorted. "I'll buy you the pants if you will take that dumb tag off."

"But sweetheart," I said, "you are paying an extra $40 for that label."

"I don't care what they cost because you look great in that style and color of pants, but that stupid tag's got to go. It detracts from the look of the pants."

With a few reservations I told him, "Okay," and we bought the pants and headed home.

I wore those slacks for weeks, but did not remove the label. After all, we had paid an extra $40 for it. Besides, wearing that label had put the youth of the church on notice that I was totally cool.

All of a sudden it hit me like a ton of bricks. Vivian Cline, you are "proud," aren't you? You can't take that label off because of your *pride*. You want the youth to think you're cool because of your label. Wouldn't you rather have them think you are cool because of who you are, than because of what you wear?

Slowly, I took that pair of pants and a seam ripper up to my desk in my office and sat down. I was so embarrassed. Pride had slipped into my life without my even noticing it. Stitch by stitch I cut the entire label off.

There in front of me was a tiny piece of cloth, one inch long and about a quarter inch wide. Small as it was, it was a measuring stick of my pride. I taped it onto my desk as a reminder not to let it happen to me again.

Clothing, when used properly, can do wonderful things for our self-esteem. Don't you feel great when you buy something new to wear, and it has that crisp look and new smell? It can make you feel energetic, and give you a fresh outlook on your problems.

Even wearing our regular clothing, when it has been freshly washed and pressed, has a tendency to make us feel better and have a healthier, more positive attitude.

Educators have found that people test better and score higher when they are clean and well dressed. Even the medical profession has acknowledged that patients tend to get well faster when they can bathe and put on fresh, clean clothes.

And, of course, we all love it when someone says, "Wow, you sure look great today!" Compliments are always welcome and tend to lift and build our self-esteem. We love to get positive recognition from our peers.

But positive recognition and compliments don't have to come from people noticing that you are wearing designer labels. Needlessly expensive tags and labels are not necessary to have you looking great. You can look great and feel great because you are wearing clean, modest, and appropriate clothing that suits you. And the "smiley face" that really makes you stand out from the crowd is not a silly emblem sewn on your shirt for a designer label, as I suggested earlier. It is the genuine smile on your face when you know who you are, and when what you wear honestly suggests that what you do is in accordance with the standards given to us by Heavenly Father.

Clothing truly is a very important element in our lives. Not only does it cover us; it is literally an extension of our personality and our moods. Our clothing makes a nonverbal statement to others about who we are and what we stand for.

It is my prayer that we will carefully select feathers that will reflect our high standards and our dedication to our Father in Heaven and his son Jesus Christ. If we choose the feathers we wear, with this in mind, then when "birds of a feather flock together," we will find ourselves in the company of those who judge people by the value of their inner selves rather than by any fine and flashy feathers that may adorn their outside. I pray that we will be an example of high standards, not only in our words and actions, but in our appearance as well.

Vivian R. Cline is the director of Brigham Young University's "Polish with Pleasure" workshops. A professional model for fifteen years, she was Mrs. Utah America in 1980. Sister Cline manages her own finishing school and is a professional speaker, often addressing business conventions. She enjoys traveling, working with youth, playing softball, and reading the scriptures. She and her husband, S. Douglas Cline, have five children.

6

FAITH IN THE LORD
AND THE YOU THE LORD SEES

MARK ELLISON

"Why is it so hard to get self-confidence?" one of my seminary students asked me recently. That's a good question, and one I've often pondered. I want to share with you some things I've learned about confidence; not *self*-confidence, however, but confidence in the Lord.

Let me begin by telling you about my daughter Kasey. Kasey is an adorable, hyper, two-and-a-half-year-old, blue-eyed, strawberry-blonde, wondrous girlful of giggles, and I love her. She's truly one of the most hilarious people I know. I was so thrilled when she first began to talk, because it meant I could finally hear what this amazing child had to say. Early on, she said "Daddy," and I beamed. Soon came, "I wuv you," and my heart swelled. But it was when she learned to ask, "Kiss it better?" that things got interesting. Suddenly, she was dashing about the house eagerly, *intentionally* inflicting minor "hurts" on herself! She'd bang an elbow or scrape a knee, then ask, "Kiss it better?" And a kiss from my wife or me would send her happily on her way, saying, "Feel better!" What a spaz!

As much as I love Kasey, however, I could do without her messy diapers. One afternoon Kasey waddled up to me, bow-legged. I sniffed. Uh oh. The Smell.

"Do you have Yuck?" I asked, as if I needed to.

I carried her to the changing table and gingerly undid her

49

diaper. Poor Kasey. Not only did she have a really messy mess, she had a stinging, neon-red, diaper rash.

"Rash, rash," she cried, and my eyes blurred with tears (more from the smell than from sympathy).

And then, as I was looking down at Her Messiness, she asked, "Kiss it better?"

I couldn't stop laughing! "I love you, Bunch," I told her, "but *no way!*"

The things she says! For instance, Kasey and I were at the local swimming pool one afternoon when she came up with another interesting statement, although this one wasn't actually funny. I was holding her afloat in the water as she kicked, and she was having a blast. "Kasey simming!" she squealed. "Kasey simming *all by self.*"

"No," I said, "Daddy is helping you."

"No. Kasey do it, *all by I self!*"

I suddenly realized how dangerous her misconception was, and I said to her, "Kasey, don't you ever, *ever* get in the water by yourself. You can't swim on your own yet. Only with Daddy or Mommy to help you, okay?"

A few weeks later we were visiting my family in California. Kasey loved that vacation, especially playing in Grandma and Grandpa's swimming pool. One day we were all outside swimming and decided to go inside for lunch. We had been in the house for a few minutes when we heard screams coming from out by the pool. Kasey! "I thought she was here with us!" everyone started to say. We dashed outside and found her standing on a step in the Jacuzzi, dripping wet, and shrieking with fear.

She had ventured alone back to the pool, and thinking she could swim, "all by self," she had jumped right in the pool. My little Bunch was completely submerged, but had somehow been able to kick her way to the steps. We thanked God she was only terribly frightened, and not drowned.

Our family narrowly avoided a tragedy that day. You can bet we watched her like hawks from then on! To this day, if you ask her, "Kasey, what happened when you jumped in Grandpa's pool?" she'll put her hands on her head and say, "Water go over head . . . scared!"

"And, are you supposed to jump in by yourself?"

"Noooo, Mommy and Daddy help you."

Let's talk about a spiritual application of what Kasey learned. As we confront challenges in our lives, some of us are prone to think, "I can do this by myself." In truth, we need the hand of God to keep us afloat. The moment we start thinking we can handle life on our own, we find ourselves in over our heads. None of us is so strong or so righteous that we don't need to depend on the Lord for help. Having faith in the Lord also means we need to *recognize* his hand in our lives, and thank him for his blessings. Just as Kasey was not aware that I was keeping her afloat, perhaps we aren't always aware of all the ways that the Lord sustains us. King Benjamin said, "O how you ought to thank your heavenly King! . . . who has created you, and has kept and preserved you, and has caused that ye should rejoice, . . . and is preserving you from day to day, by lending you breath, that ye may live . . . " (Mosiah 2:19–21).

I went down to Lake Powell a couple of years ago to compete in a triathlon. The race consisted of a one-mile swim, twenty-five miles of cycling, and 6.2 miles of running. In triathlons, you go from one event directly to the next, with no time-outs. I had trained long and hard to prepare for this one. I even discussed the course with another triathlete who had previously competed in the Lake Powell race.

"Hot and hilly," he said ominously, "and watch out for the cattle guard."

You know what a cattle guard is. It's that big metal grate set into the highway to keep cows from wandering off their range. Driving over one of those in a car really shakes you up, but trying to pedal a little racing bike with skinny tires across one is downright dangerous.

This triathlete went on to explain, "The bike course is out-and-back. On the way out, you climb a big hill. On the way back, you come back down. At the bottom of the hill there's a cattle guard and some rough road. I came down that thing at light-speed, and when I hit the cattle guard, I flew off the bike, and skidded forever. I was total 'road meat,' man. It was weeks before I got out of the hospital. Never have been the same since."

Gulp. I stood there listening, sort of wishing I hadn't already paid the entry fee.

When I got to the lake the night before the race, I got my first look at Killer Hill. Silhouetted against the desert sky like a giant Tyrannosaurus Rex, it seemed to be growling at me. It said, "I'm eating you for breakfast in the morning."

At the pre-race meeting, we were told there would be plywood over the cattle guard to make it safe, but I was still nervous. As I prayed before going to sleep that night, my request "that no harm or injury would befall me" had real meaning. I always get some pre-race jitters, but this time, I was *scared*.

The race began at 7:30 A.M., and we were off, into the lake. I swam as hard as I could, and as I exited the water, people shouted that I was in fourth place. I peeled off my wetsuit, donned a helmet and sunglasses, and took off on the bike. Up Killer Hill, then out onto the highway I went. My legs were burning and my lungs felt like they were about to jump out of my throat! I didn't think I could catch the leaders, but I hoped I could hold on for a top-five finish. When I reached the turnaround point, I was still in fourth place. A few more miles of cranking, and I finally reached the top of the back side of Killer Hill. I began my descent, shifting into my biggest gear combination so I could reach maximum speed. Soon I was pedalling as fast as my gears could go. Completely spun out, I got down in an aerodynamic tuck, and picked up even more speed. Images flew by in a blur to my right and my left. Onlookers yelled, "Go for it!" I risked a glance at my bike computer. It read *52 miles per hour!* As I approached the bottom of the hill, I saw the cattle guard, and—horror of horrors!— the plywood plank was way off to the side, in the gravel, on the shoulder of the road! I spent the next millisecond contemplating what would happen if I tried to steer through loose gravel on narrow racing tires while going 52 miles an hour. Needless to say, I ruled out that option. The cattle guard drew nearer, and I began to brace myself for disaster. But at the last moment, a thought occurred to me: *Bunny hop the cattle guard.*

In cycling, there's this technique called the "bunny hop." You pull up on your handlebars, lifting your front wheel off the road, and at just the right moment, you also pull up with your feet, which are locked onto the pedals with ski-type bindings. You can lift your entire bike off the ground for a moment. If you're good at it, and your timing is right, you can clear pot holes, speed bumps, and even railroad tracks. I wasn't very good at it. I had never been able to get the timing right! I would always come down right on top of the speed bump—CRASH! (That *hurts*, by the way.) And this cattle guard was wider across than railroad tracks, quite a distance to jump! But there was no alternative—bunny hop the beast, or become "road meat."

So, just as I got to the huge grate in the road—its metal bars stretched out like enormous fangs ready to eat me alive—with spectators and race volunteers screaming, "WATCH OUT!" I pulled up on the handlebars and lifted my feet. . . .

Slow motion: Bicycle and rider are launched into the air, gliding through a gentle arc, clearing the cattle guard, and then touching down, . . . SMOOTH AS SILK. Woosh! And I was flying safely down the road towards town, while behind me the spectators on the side of the road were standing with their mouths agape.

Then they were cheering and clapping.

"Whooee! Did you *see* that, man?!"

There never had been such a flawless jump, such a clean, easy landing; nay, not even in the annals of the *Tour de France.*

Adrenaline shot through me, and I began to laugh insanely, out loud! I was so pumped!

I rolled into the transition area, quickly changed into running shoes, charged through the run (during which I unfortunately was passed by this one total motorhead runner), and finished the race in 5th place. I had reached my goal! I felt *great.* At the finish line, I stood around with the others in the prestigious top five. We chatted about the race and our training, and sort of stroked one another's egos with comments like, "You had a great swim, man," and, "Dude, you *flew* by me on the run, no kidding, I felt *wind*," and so on. Male bonding. And finally I could resist the urge to brag no longer.

"So," I said casually, "did you guys bunny hop that cattle guard?"

"What??" they asked.

"You know, that cattle guard at the bottom of the hill. Did you bunny hop the mama, too?"

They looked at me incredulously.

"No way, man. We slowed down and took the plywood. *We* weren't going to get killed! Did *you* hop it?"

I nodded coolly. They shook their heads. They called me a madman. They spoke in whispers. My head swelled with pride!

A few days later, still feeling quite cocky from my little triumph (and may I add here that it feels oh, so good to hear people cheer for you when you successfully bunny hop a cattle guard at 52 miles an hour), I happened to be reading the scriptures. I came upon this verse, and felt an immediate sting of rebuke: "And in nothing doth man offend God, or against none is his wrath kindled, save *those who confess not his hand in all things*, and obey not his commandments" (Doctrine & Covenants 59:21; italics added).

Oops! I thought about my attitude. I had not confessed the hand of God in my race. Now, I don't know that angels were dispatched from heaven for the purpose of carrying me over that grate in the road. But what had I prayed for? Safety. No harm or accident. And then I had encountered a dangerous situation, and had come through it unscathed, with a performance beyond my usual ability. Perhaps I didn't need to speculate on God's role in that as much as I *did* need to say thank you, humbly, and sincerely. I did so, and ever since then I have tried continually to express proper gratitude for the Lord's helping hand.

We need to confess God's hand in all things, not because God really needs our thanks, but because *we* need always to remember that *he is the source*; the source of all power, the source of help and direction for us, the means by whom salvation becomes a possibility. As Paul said, "I can do all things *through Christ which strengtheneth me"* (Philippians 4:13; italics added). Even Ammon, the mighty missionary, confessed, "I know that I am nothing; as to my strength I am weak; therefore I will not boast of myself, but I will boast of my God, for *in his strength* I can do all things" (Alma 26:12; italics added).

Listen to successful returned missionaries talk, and you'll notice they speak, not about how many people *they* converted, but of the miracles *the Lord* worked in their lives, and in the lives of others. Real, enduring confidence doesn't come through great accomplishments that make us look good. Confidence comes when we discover how to have faith in the Lord.

Why do we need to have faith in Jesus? First, because he is the author of *salvation.* Jesus has provided a way for us to be *saved* from both physical and spiritual death. Through his atonement everyone will be resurrected, and each of us may also gain forgiveness of our sins by truly repenting and enduring in faith. But the power of Jesus to bless our lives is not all in the future. He extends himself into our daily lives, and will assist us in our day-to-day struggles as well. I sometimes feel that many LDS youth mistakenly think the atonement is only useful when someone commits a really bad sin. An understanding that Jesus is a daily source of strength provides a whole new perspective, and enables us to face life's challenges more confidently. Let's consider lack of confidence. Do you, like my seminary student, sometimes feel insecure, not good enough, talented enough, popular enough, smart enough, or funny enough? There's nothing unusual about having those kinds of feelings; in fact, everybody struggles with them. Welcome to the club—The Inadequate-Low-Confidence-Humans-Association (ILCHA). Some of the greatest heroes of all time have been members in good standing of ILCHA.

I'd like to introduce you to three prominent members. First, meet Enoch. The Lord said, "Prophesy unto this people," and Enoch replied, "You've got to be kidding, Lord. No one's going to listen to me. I'm just an ugly little freshman and I'm totally unpopular." Actually, his exact words were, "[I] am but a lad, and all the people hate me" (Moses 6:27, 31). But there is another club this unloved lad became a member of: The I-Will-Go-and-

Do-It-Anyway Society (IWGADIAS?). In his heart, Enoch knew, like Nephi did, that God doesn't give his children commandments that are impossible to keep. Instead, he "prepare[s] a way for them that they may accomplish the thing which he commandeth them" (1 Nephi 3:7). The Lord knew Enoch, saw what he could be, and reassured him, saying, "No man shall pierce thee" (Moses 6:32). Enoch believed. He went on to become one of the greatest leaders in the history of the earth. In the process, Enoch discovered that not everyone hated him, but that there were many good people who would accept him. "So great was the faith of Enoch that he led the people of God" (Moses 7:13). And what's the first thing that comes to the minds of most Latter-day Saints when they hear the name Enoch? Zion! The City of Holiness that was taken up into heaven, the city full of people who followed Enoch, the city where everyone was "of one heart and one mind, and dwelt in righteousness [with] no poor among them" (Moses 7:18). Feel unpopular? Be your true, righteous, humble self, and ask the Lord to help you find good friends.

Next, meet Moses. Did you know that he, too, lacked self-confidence? Remember, there's no sin in that. In fact, "It is better to trust in the Lord than to put confidence in man" (Psalm 118:8). The question is, how do we *deal* with our insecurity? Do we trust in the Lord to help us? Moses did. When he faced the prospect of confronting the king of Egypt and the task of leading Israel out of bondage, he asked, "Who am I, that I should go unto Pharaoh, and that I should bring forth the children of Israel out of Egypt? . . . O my Lord, I am not eloquent . . . but I am slow of speech" (Exodus 3:11; 4:10). Have you ever faced a task like having to give a talk in church? You can probably empathize with Moses' fear of public speaking. (Shoot, it still makes *me* nervous!) But the Lord reminded Moses, "Who hath made man's mouth? . . . Have not I the Lord?" (Exodus 4:11). Remember, the Lord has created *worlds without number.* Can't he create a mighty prophet out of a man who is a little "slow of speech"? Easily! Can he help us achieve *our* missions in life, even though we each have weaknesses? No sweat. He can. And will. If we'll only let him. That means we must do our part.

Look at Ether 12:27 where the Lord assures us, "My grace is sufficient for all men that humble themselves before me; for if they humble themselves before me, and have faith in me, then will I make weak things become strong unto them." The Bible Dictionary explains, "grace is an *enabling power*" (p. 697, italics added). Because Moses was humble and faithful, the Lord *enabled* him to accomplish his mission, and assured him, "I, the Almighty, have chosen thee, and thou shalt be made stronger than many waters; for they shall obey thy command" (Moses 1:25). The Lord knew Moses also, and saw what he could be, too. And today, what do you think of when you hear the name Moses? If you're like me, you think of that dramatic moment at the Red Sea, when he experienced literal fulfillment of the promise, "thou shalt be made stronger than many waters." There on the shore, he and hundreds of thousands of Israelites found themselves with no course of retreat as the massive Egyptian army stampeded toward them. "Good going, Moses," the Israelites started to say, "you led us out here to die." But then, filled with inspiration, this man who had once complained, "I am not eloquent," raised his voice over the roaring of the crowd, and spoke these powerful words: "Fear ye not; stand still, and see the salvation of the Lord" (Exodus 14:13). Miraculously, the sea parted, and the children of Israel walked through on dry ground.

The Lord really does "prepare a way"! Are you weak in some ways? Your most embarrassing weaknesses can become your greatest strengths, but not if you try to do it on your own. Though human willpower is strong, it's not enough. Do your best to become stronger, then beg the Lord to bless and assist you.

Do you feel like life is tough? Meet our third hero. At age seven, he nearly drowned. Not long after that, his face was disfigured by a paralyzing disease. While still a boy, his sister and his mother died. As a young man, he contracted smallpox. Later, he would have his tonsils out, and then for fifteen years would suffer from recurring boils on his nose, lips, and waist. Then, one day he was called to be an apostle. Do you know what his first words were? "I am so weak and small and limited and incapable . . . I can't do it" (Edward L. Kimball and Andrew E. Kimball,

Jr., *Spencer W. Kimball* [Salt Lake City: Bookcraft, 1977], pp. 189–90.) But the Lord knew Spencer Kimball, and saw what he could be, too. The Lord reassured him, and he accepted the calling. During President Kimball's service as a General Authority, the Church grew and progressed as it never had before. Yet throughout that entire time, his trials continued: biopsies, throat cancer, surgeries, chest pains, open-heart surgery, another attack of the paralyzing Bell's palsy, skin cancer, and on and on. All of these things failed to discourage him, and they combined to give him profound understanding:

> Though I know God has a major role in our lives, I do not know how much he causes to happen and how much he merely permits. Whatever the answer to this question, there is another I feel sure about. Could the Lord have prevented these tragedies? The answer is, Yes. The Lord is omnipotent, with all power to control our lives, save us pain, prevent all accidents, . . . save us from labor, effort, sickness, even from death, if he will. But he will not. (Spencer W. Kimball, *Faith Precedes the Miracle* [Salt Lake City: Deseret Book, 1973], p. 96.)

Spencer W. Kimball wasn't angry at God. He understood that to be shielded from all trials would destroy free agency, and therefore, the testing and learning purposes of this life. He had faith that God would never allow us to be tried more than we are able to bear (see 1 Corinthians 10:13). When trials come, remember that they are manageable, with the Lord's help.

The faithless ask, "Why did God do this?" The faithful ask, "God, help me through this." People mean well when they say, "Have confidence in yourself—you can do it!" But, a better approach is: "Have confidence in the Lord, and if it is right, *you and the Lord* can surely do it." The world teaches us to put our trust in ourselves, in money, in power, in science, in nothing at all, if you please. The scriptures teach: Put your faith in the Lord, and he will show you who you really are, and what this life is all about.

The Lord Jesus Christ knows you, and sees what *you* can be. He has given you some guidelines that will help get you there, that will help you become what you are meant to become. Those guidelines are the commandments—standards that may seem hard to live by sometimes. But, join with the heroes who went and did it anyway.

Tell yourself, "I *will* live differently from the world. I don't know how I'll make it, but I won't be alone—the Lord's hand will keep me afloat." The First Presidency has said, "[God] has promised to help you as you live gospel standards" (*For the Strength of Youth*, p. 19). He *will* help you!

Tell yourself, "I *will* stay morally clean, despite the immorality of the world around me." Then do your part—abide by Church standards, and "watch and pray continually, that ye may not be tempted above that which ye can bear" (Alma 13:28). And in the process, watch the Lord enable you with the strong confidence that he bestows on those who "let virtue garnish [their] thoughts unceasingly" (Doctrine & Covenants 121:45). It *will* happen!

Young men, tell yourselves, "I *will* serve a mission," and then prepare. You'll go out and experience first-hand the Lord's promise to missionaries: "I will be on your right hand and on your left, and my Spirit shall be in your hearts, and mine angels round about you, to bear you up" (Doctrine & Covenants 84:88).

I pray that the Holy Ghost will enlighten your mind and help you truly understand these words. What I have shared with you is a basic, plain, and precious principle. In fact, it's the *first* principle of the gospel—Faith in the Lord Jesus Christ (see Article of Faith 4). Christ our Savior loves us, wants to help us, and has power to do so, if we'll let him. It's that simple. May your faith in the Lord grow, so that you can overcome weaknesses, resist temptations, endure trials, repent of transgressions, accomplish what the Lord would have you accomplish, and ultimately be "received into heaven, that thereby [you] may dwell with God in a state of never-ending happiness" (Mosiah 2:41). You and the Lord can surely do it.

Mark Ellison is a seminary instructor in Springville, Utah. A former American sign language teacher at Brigham Young University and at the MTC, Brother Ellison has also served as a director of Especially for Deaf Youth. Mark has held "tons of odd jobs," from night janitor, to a guitarist in a dance band, to a swimming pool digger. He enjoys triathlon racing, and he and his wife, Lauren, have two children.

ALL FOR THE LOVE OF A FRIEND

STEPHEN JASON HALL

One of the most incredible institutions in the world is friendship. It is one that continually baffles and astounds me. I have searched often for its definition and I have found two that describe it better than any others I have heard. Before we talk about these definitions, take a minute to think of your best friends. How do you feel when you are around them? Who or what do they motivate you to become? And how are you inspired to be, because of their influence?

The first of the two definitions, I initially read on the chalkboard in my sixth-grade classroom. My teacher firmly believed in the power of positive peer pressure and the effect for good it could have on his students. He would begin each day by writing a quotation on the board, and we would copy it into a notebook that he hoped we would keep throughout our lives. This particular day, I entered the following words into my notebook, words that I would never forget: "A friend is someone who walks in when the rest of the world walks out." I found the second quote on friendship while reading the scriptures. It reinforces the definition I learned in the sixth grade, and simply says, "A friend loveth at all times" (Proverbs 17:17).

As I think of my friends, and how they fare against such a standard, I am inclined to divide them into three categories — my peers, my family, and my God.

It was a hot, dry July afternoon in Colorado when the helicopter life-flighted me from Lake Powell, Utah, where I had been seriously injured in a diving accident, to the St. Mary's hospital in Grand Junction, Colorado, where I was to receive the life-saving care that I so urgently needed. They took me from the helipad to the emergency room where I underwent numerous tests. The doctor concluded that I was paralyzed, due to a broken neck. In order to confirm the diagnosis, I was to have a Cat Scan. I remember lying in that large white tube, as scared as I have ever been in my entire life. I didn't know if I would ever walk again. Yet, interestingly enough, the number-one question in my mind was not whether I would live or die, but who would be my friend? I wondered, "Who would want to go to a dance with a guy in a wheelchair? Who would want to date a guy in a wheelchair? Who would want to go to parties, basketball games, or youth activities with a guy in a wheelchair? Who would be able to look past my chair and see a living, breathing person?" How excited I was with the answer that I received.

After a three-week stay in Colorado, I was moved to the University of Utah hospital in Salt Lake City, Utah. I was very excited about this move because my hometown of Boise, Idaho, was only six hours away and I would finally be able to see my friends. I vividly remember the day when my best friend came to see me. When Jonah came into my room, I guess I was quite a sight to behold — six-foot-three, and one hundred and eighteen pounds! You could see every bone and joint in my body. Tubes were coming out of everywhere imaginable and I bore more metal than Robocop. All of this, coupled with that familiar hospital smell, was more than Jonah could handle. He looked at me, his eyes glazed over, and as he said, "Hi, Jason. How are you doing?" . . . SMACK!! he hit the floor. He had passed out, as cold as a cucumber.

I yelled for the nurses. "HELP! HELP!" They ran in, stood on top of Jonah, peered at me with alarm, and frantically asked, "What's the matter?"

I explained that they were standing on "the matter," and embarrassed, they jumped off him, and excused themselves ever so politely. They gave Jonah some smelling salts, sat him in a chair, made sure he was coherent enough to know where he was, and then sent him home.

Two weeks later, Jonah returned. I couldn't believe it, I was so excited. He walked in, took a look at me, inhaled a nose full of the smell, got a glassy look in his eye, said, "Hi, Jason. How are you?" and . . . SMACK!! He hit the floor again.

I yelled for the nurses, they came in, took one look at Jonah, and said, "Oh *him* again." They gave him some smelling salts, and Jonah left.

I appreciated the concern that Jonah had shown me, and I really wanted to talk to him, but I just didn't think he would come back for another "visit." However, just two weeks later, there he was, and the ritual began again. Jonah saw me, took in the aroma, and was on his way to the floor. Only this time, the nurses had followed him in, smelling salts in hand, fully prepared to catch him. Three times Jonah had come to see me, and three times he had spent nearly as much time on the floor as he had with me. Yet, none of that mattered to Jonah. What mattered to him was that I knew he cared and in our short visits, he changed my life. Many of my other friends weren't able to accept my disability. It was hard for them to show that they cared. But Jonah, and other friends like him, demonstrated true friendship by walking in when the rest of the world walked out.

Can we be like Jonah? I believe that we can by taking a few minutes out of our everyday lives to let another know that we care. When we do, we will come closer to finding out what friendship truly is. For to have a good friend, we must be one; and to have our lives changed, we must change another's.

My family has also had a profound effect on my life. I have never found a group of people more committed to me and to my salvation than my family. Only within the family can we find unconditional love here on earth. When I think of the special relationships that I enjoy in my own family, I am reminded of two examples. First is my mother. After a person breaks his neck, paralysis is not the only difficulty that ensues. There are breathing problems, skin care concerns, and your body thermostat goes way out of whack. You are either really hot or really cold, but never comfortable. Directly after my injury I was hot, extremely hot, and in order to keep me cool the nurses placed every fan and air conditioner they could get their hands on in my room. The temperature in the room helped me, but made it uncomfortable for visitors. In spite of this, Mom spent time with me. She would walk to the hospital, in the heat of a Colorado July, wearing two shirts, a sweater, and carrying a shawl. She would arrive at 8:30 A.M. and stay with me until the end of visiting hours, only to return the next morning. She did this all day, every day, for three months. And for the next year-and-a-half she spent her days caring for me. Waking up at 5:00 A.M. to get me ready for my 7:00 A.M. class, she would take me there, only to pick me up an hour later to take me to a two- to three-hour session of therapy. Then she would put me back into the car and rush me back to school for my 2:00 P.M. class. After class, she would pick me up, take me home, feed me, and put me down for the night. Then she would prepare to do it all over again the next day. It was a lot of work — work that others would have refused, but work that she accepted because she loved me. It didn't matter what the job was, or how hard it was, she loved me, and so she would do it, and without complaint. Her love is a love that is irreplaceable and unconditional.

The second example is my sweet wife, Kolette. During my stay in the hospital, there were nights when I wondered if anyone would ever be able to look beyond all of the metal, to see into my soul, and love me for who I was. How grateful I am to have found a girl who loves me enough to accept my handicap as her own, and who continues to battle the situation with me. By definition, friends are those who give us strength and buoy us up in time of need. If this is the case, then she is truly my finest friend. For it is her love that gives me the courage to get up in the morning and fight another day.

What I find interesting is that we often listen least to those we love the most. I remember that, as a young boy, I loved to swim. And one of my mom's good friends had a pool. So, I naturally loved to go with her to visit her friend. On one such occasion, we pulled into the driveway, and even before the car came to a full stop, I flew from the car and ran into the house. I knew that I had to say "Hello," before I could swim. After quickly greeting our gracious hostess, and with Mom's permission, I was on my way toward the patio. Mom warned me to watch out for the sliding glass door as I bolted for the pool. I wasn't especially interested in what she said, for I had just gotten a new pair of white tennis shoes, and so was therefore moving especially fast—too fast to pay attention to Mom's warning. There was . . . the pool! It looked so cool, so blue, and so enticing, and getting every ounce of speed out of my new shoes, I leapt for the pool. And WHAM! I hit the glass door and fell to the floor, unconscious. Finally I awoke, not much in the mood to swim, and wishing I had listened to my mom.

Do we ever put ourselves in a similar situation? Often the loved ones in our families have a perspective that we don't. And as we speed through life, we don't always see the invisible glass doors that lie in our way. From the vantage point of their experience, parents can frequently warn us of such pitfalls. If we heed their advice we can avoid many problems we might otherwise stumble into. If we don't heed their warnings, we can find ourselves flat on our backs, knocked out cold.

Even though this is all true, there still may be times when we will be abandonned by our finest friends, and yes, maybe even by our families. But, there is one friend who will never leave us, and that is Jesus Christ.

During my freshman year at Brigham Young University, I was lonely, very lonely. And, as the time passed, it wasn't getting any better. My roommate was very popular, especially with the girls, and that just made things worse. One night, I had had enough. I needed to find out, I needed to know if anyone cared. So, I left our dorm and went to a place where I could be alone. I went to a little spot just above the Provo Temple. It was sunset and the lights on the temple and in the city were just beginning to come up. I found myself deep in prayer. I fervently asked my Father in Heaven to let me know that he cared, that he loved me, and that I was his son. The answer I received is one that I will never forget. His spirit touched mine and let me know that he loved me, that he was my friend. After that, I knew that no matter what anyone else thought, I was special to him. What a privilege it was for me to know that I could be his friend, and how grateful I have been for that knowledge. However, we should not assume that this privilege is simply given and not to be earned. We quote the scripture "Greater love hath no man than this, that a man lay down his life for his friends," and because we know that he gave his life for us, we *assume* that he is our friend. Yet, it is the following verse of scripture that is important. He says, "Ye are my friends, if ye do whatsoever I command you" (John 15:12–14). We can be his friends only if we keep his commandments. The following are representative of some of the commandments that we can keep to come close to him.

We must read the scriptures. President Benson has made this one of the keynotes of his presidency, especially encouraging us to read the Book of Mormon. He has done this for a good reason. The Book of Mormon is "Another Testament of Jesus Christ" (see title page), and Joseph Smith said that we can come nearer to God by reading it than we can by any other book. As we learn more of the Savior, by reading the accounts and witnesses of those who already know him—the prophets for whom he was a reality—we may come to know him ourselves. Then, knowing him, we can become his friends.

We must pray, and do so diligently. If we hope to come close to anyone we must communicate with them. What an opportunity we have, any time we choose, to speak to the Most High God. Doesn't it seem wondrous that at *our* convenience we may call upon Heavenly Father, and be certain we will have his attention? This time is precious, and we must make it count. We must let him know who we are, what is important to us, what we are thankful for, and what we stand in need of. By regularly offering such prayers we will establish a relationship, not only with the Father, but with the Son, in whose name we offer our prayers.

We must take seriously the promise that we make to him weekly as we gather at the sacrament table. There, we promise to keep his commandments, and to always remember him. Think of the effect it would have in our lives if we were successful in keeping the Savior in our minds during all of our waking hours! Think of the effect it would have in our lives if we made it our goal to always be in situations where he would not be reluctant to be. By agreeing to take upon us his name, we commit to represent him in all that we say or do—our actions reflect directly on our Savior. We ought to ask ourselves at the end of each day, "How have I represented Jesus Christ today?" It is my humble prayer that we will always do so honorably. Then, in return for our pledge of allegiance to him, he promises us we will always have his Spirit to be with us—to strengthen, guide, and encourage us. What a promise!

So, the question becomes, how much are you willing to do in order to establish this kind of relationship with the Savior?—to enjoy his Spirit and to be counted as his "friend"? Are you willing to relinquish all dishonesty? Are you willing to keep the Word of Wisdom? Are you willing to pass over R-rated movies? And are you willing to live a morally clean life? If we wish to be his friends, we must make just such decisions. The exciting thing is that when you do make and keep such a commitment, you will know that when he said, "Greater love hath no man than this, that a man lay down his life for his friends" (John 15:13), he had you in mind—that you are numbered among the friends of the Savior.

Stephen Jason Hall is a student at Brigham Young University who grew up in Idaho. An Eagle Scout, Jason was junior class president and a member of his seminary council while in high school. While attending BYU, he served as an executive director in student government, on the Honor Code Committee, and as student-body president. He enjoys music, public speaking, drama, basketball, and BYU football.

8

REAL LOVE – THE MOST AWESOME ADVENTURE

SUZANNE L. HANSEN

I heard of a young man who had such a great need to be loved by a particular young lady that he sent her a special delivery letter every day for sixty days. On the sixty-first day, she announced she was in love with the mailman and that they would marry.

All joking aside, let's face it. Most of us have a strong, overwhelming need to be loved. Love is needed in order to survive, and we need it from our earliest beginnings. Countless studies have shown that human babies need to be held, cuddled, and spoken to lovingly, from the moment of birth. When they are loved, people grow and mature into healthy adults. Without it, they may sicken both physically and emotionally, and may even die. Love is as important to our health and well-being as good food.

In my experience with young people, I have discovered that many feel like Bennett Cerf in the following story.

Some years ago, a number of famous men and women were on a TV talk show discussing the things that made them most afraid. They agreed that they were afraid of powerful weapons that could annihilate the world. They also feared energy shortages, crime in the cities, and world pollution.

During most of the discussion one man remained silent. Bennett Cerf, a journalist and TV commentator, was usually a very talkative man. That day, he sat very quietly, contributing nothing.

Just as the show was about to end, the host said, "Well, Mr. Cerf, you haven't said much. Isn't there anything you really fear?"

In a quiet voice, Bennett Cerf answered, "There's really only one thing I really fear — and that's not being loved."

We all crave love, just like plants crave water. And we do all sorts of funny, ridiculous, crazy, noble, special things to earn the love of other people. We also sing, dance, write, play an instrument, or participate in some kind of sport — and we do it partly for the approval of others and the applause of the crowd.

Basically, there are takers and there are givers of love. Takers fear they won't have love. Albert Einstein once said, "We're either full of love, or full of fear."

Takers seem to demand love, and tend to draw it from others, without offering any in return. Have you ever been around anyone like that? You might hear a taker say, "Why haven't you called me lately? I've been waiting to hear from you." These people want the loving feeling that comes from knowing that another friend wants to talk to them, but they do not see the need to call that friend.

Have you been around people who "hog" a conversation with repeated stories about *their* school, friends, people at work, clothes, and dates? Very quickly we are boxed out of the conversation while our friend is intoxicated with himself or herself, glancing up only to make sure that someone is still listening.

Such people often have low self-esteem, and they seek the admiration and attention of others in order to feel worthwhile. Ultimately, they push so hard for this attention and acceptance that no one can stand to be their friend. It seems strange, doesn't it, when all along all they wanted was to be loved.

Some people learn to rely upon the feelings they derive from using drugs, alcohol, and premarital sex, as substitutes for real love. All of these provide a false sense of well-being, but the effects are only temporary and not truly fulfilling.

Then there are the benefits that come to the givers of love. I've found that the one sure way of getting love is to give it. It's been said that life gives to the giver and takes from the taker. I believe that a lost opportunity to give love is a lost opportunity to receive love.

The story is told about a young man who was having a difficult time. He decided to take a break from his troubles and visit someone who needed a lift. He walked into a convalescent home, made his way to the desk, and asked if he might see anyone who could use a visit. He approached those people and said with a smile, "Hello, I'm the offical hugger around here. I've just come to share a bit of sunshine. I'd like to give you a hug."

The older people loved getting a hug. This sincere young man made them feel loved, vital, and alive. And in return, he felt worthwhile and loved. As he was leaving, many reached out, and grabbed and kissed his hand, as tears streamed down their cheeks. As he drove home, his burdens seemed lighter.

Even though we all want to be loved, we sometimes forget the simple things we can do to *give* love. These steps will bring more abundant love into your life as you give love:

STEP 1 – SPEAK LOVING WORDS

When we're kind and tender in the way we talk with others, whether they are strangers or closely related to us, we are offering them love.

Unfortunately, people often abuse each other with harsh words. Remember, we are known to others, perhaps more than anything else, *by the words we speak*. Having a positive, loving attitude, when speaking to anyone, can brighten some of the darkest days.

Al Sizer lives in Portland, Oregon. He decided to go out to eat at an excellent restaurant called Daiseys. When Al arrived, the line for a table was already a half-block long, so he agreed to sit at the counter. Sitting next to him was a downcast, withdrawn man who apparently didn't want to be disturbed.

But Al has a wonderful, effervescent, positive personality and he began talking to the man and finally broke through his shell. They talked together for almost two hours. Then Al realized he had an appointment, gave his business card to the man, and left, never expecting to hear from him again.

The next week the man from the restaurant came to Al's office with tears in his eyes, saying, "Al, you saved my life."

Al was flabbergasted. The man poured out his story. Just hours before they had met at Daiseys, a doctor had told this man that his X rays showed he had a terminal illness, one that would prove to be very painful toward the end. On the spot, the fellow had decided to commit suicide, rather than have to experience such a horrible death. But he decided to first have one last meal at his favorite restaurant. And that's how he came to be at Daiseys, where he met Al.

Al had spoken to him so kindly and affirmatively about families and caring, that he had decided not to end his life that day, and not to deprive his wife and children of the few months that might be left to him.

A week later, he had gone back to the doctor, and had learned that somehow his X rays had been switched or mixed-up with someone else's. He didn't actually have the illness he had feared. If he had not had that conversation with Al, he would have ended his life.

We never know what effect a soft, kind word will have on another person, or how important a listening ear will be to someone else. Just caring enough to give the "I care" message may be all that is needed to even save a life.

STEP 2 – WRITING LOVE NOTES

A love note is an excellent way to communicate love to another person. When the person receives it, he or she will feel warm and loved. And you will feel better for having written it.

Notes can be hidden to be found in purses, pockets, lockers, cupboards, pillows, or in other fun, unexpected places. Several weeks after my uncle died, his wife found a love note he had written to her and hidden in a place she would look when she was cleaning. It touched her deeply and helped her feel close to him in her time of loss.

Love notes are vitally important, especially to grandparents, friends, or loved ones who, just like you, need a lift. Teachers and others who serve us also need to know how much we appreciate them.

As a man lay on his deathbed, his wife said, "Dear, all these years we have lived together, and not once have you ever told me that you loved me — not a note, not a flower, not even a word. Am I not worthy of your love?"

He explained, "I told you I loved you on the day we got married, and I didn't think I needed to repeat myself."

No one can hear too many loving thoughts or enough kind words.

STEP 3 — GIVE A HUG

A national hug survey was reported by Mark Victor Hansen, author of *Dare to Win*. In that survey it was discovered that 83 percent of the people surveyed grew up getting less than a hug a day. Even if we are reluctant to admit it out loud, 99 percent of us want more hugs.

Dr. Dean McGraine, a psychologist, suggested that everyone needs a minimum of four hugs a day. The requirement for maximum emotional growth is twelve hugs a day. If your family members initially resist your hugs, just explain to them you're involved in a special high-tech hugging experiment — that you would like them to be the co-hugger with you for twelve hugs a day. Explain that hugging has positive effects on people. It has been shown to increase the rate of language development, I.Q., and self-esteem.

Remember, you aren't making a sexual statement by giving a hug. You're making a statement about human love and caring. In the language of my Scandinavian forefathers, the Norse word *hugga* means "to comfort, hold close, or to console."

Sometimes it's wise to ask permission to give a hug. Some people have a hard time accepting them. Even though they really need them, they may not be accustomed to either receiving or giving them. But they'll love it.

STEP 4 — ACT WITH LOVE

Actions speak louder than any words. If you care about people, how do you show your love?

On a rainy day in New York, around the turn of the century, a dishevelled, older lady stepped into a department store to get out of the weather. She asked several people for help.

Because she was dripping wet and appeared to be penniless, no one wanted to bother with her. Everyone seemed to be irritated by her, except for one young salesman who said, "Would you like a chair while you wait for someone to come and pick you up?" And then he arranged for a taxi for her.

Before she left she said, "Young man, please write down your name and address on a piece of paper and give it to me." And he did so. The next day, Andrew Carnegie, this lady's son and one of the richest men in the world at that time, called the store. He said that he wanted to buy enough furniture to fill a Scottish castle he had just purchased. And he said that he wanted to make certain the commission on the sale went to the young man who had treated his mother so kindly. Furthermore, he was inviting the young man to accompany the family to Scotland to help arrange the furnishings in the castle.

The manager of the store protested, and said he was fearful the young salesman didn't have enough experience to handle such an assignment. Mr. Carnegie disagreed, saying, "My mother said the young man treated her with great care and kindness, even though he didn't know who she was. With that kind of concern, he'll care enough to do the job correctly.

STEP 5 — SMILE

A smile — a simple smile — is like the warmth of the sun. It has the power to brighten a person's entire day — sometimes an entire life. It sends a message of your love and is a mirror to your soul. So smile often: In elevators. At people in cars. In stores. At classmates. At sales clerks. And, especially, at your family members.

More often than not, your smile will be returned, and not only will you have made someone else's day just a bit brighter, yours will be brighter as well.

ONE LAST THOUGHT ON GIVING

People who are busy loving others don't have much time to brood on whether others love them or not. Remember, love is available in abundance, if we give our love away.

An example of this great truth is found in the book *Dare to Win,* by Mark Victor Hansen. Linda Birtish, an accomplished artist and poet, died at the young age of twenty-eight, of a brain tumor. She had never married, but had drawn a picture in her last days of what she imagined her ideal man would have looked like. Perhaps some of you will recall seeing this story on the television show "20/20."

In a final act of love, she arranged to give herself away. She donated all the useful parts of her body to be used in transplants. Her eyes went to an eye bank in Bethesda, Maryland, and from there to a recipient in South Carolina. A twenty-eight-year-old man was given the gift of sight by Linda's gift of love.

He was profoundly grateful, and wrote to the eye bank to thank them for the good work they do. (Incidentally, this "love note" was only the second thank-you note they had received from a recipient of any of the over 30,000 eyes they had processed.)

But this grateful fellow wanted to go even further. He wanted to thank Linda's parents for her, and for her generous act of love and service. There was an immediate bond of love established between the young man and Linda's folks, and they invited him to stay in their home for the weekend.

He slept in Linda's room, where he noticed that some of her favorite books were the ones he had learned to enjoy in braille. The next morning, Linda's mother made the comment that he looked familiar. She was sure she had seen him somewhere before.

Remembering, Linda's mother then ran upstairs and pulled out the last picture that her artist-daughter had ever drawn. It was a picture of her ideal man, and the likeness was virtually identical to the man who had received her eyes. Then her mother read him the last poem Linda had written, even on her deathbed. It read:

Two hearts passing in the night
Falling in love
Never able to gain each other's sight.

One of the most beautiful scriptures about love was written by Moroni as he was closing the Book of Mormon. He wrote of the "pure love of Christ" which is at the root of all that is good in our world (see Moroni 7:47). Moroni saw what happened to his people because they didn't have this charity.

And for us, may we strive for this love every day. The apostle Paul described it clearly. "Charity suffereth long, and is kind; charity envieth not; charity vaunteth not itself, is not puffed up. Doth not behave itself unseemly, seeketh not her own, is not easily provoked, thinketh no evil; Rejoiceth not in iniquity, but rejoiceth in the truth"(1 Corinthians 13:4–6).

Such love, Paul said, "never faileth" (v. 8). Now, that's *real* love!

Follow the five simple steps I've outlined, and you will feel love flooding into your life, as you give it to others. What an awesome adventure! You will have nothing to fear, and you will be numbered among the elect of God.

Suzanne L. Hansen is a lecturer and a businesswoman in Salt Lake City. Suzanne has worked as a newspaper columnist, appeared on many TV talk shows, and has authored five books. She has several times been named one of the Outstanding Young Women in America. A former college homecoming queen, she enjoys arts and crafts, flower arrangement, classical music, and new age music. Sister Hansen and her husband, Michael, have three children.

9

HAMBURGERS, FRIES, PIES, AND A SOFT DRINK— OR DARE TO DO RIGHT!

VICTOR HARRIS

During my years as a cemetery, I mean, seminary instructor, I have observed that the two toughest challenges teenagers face are: (1) to stand up to peers in peer pressure situations; and (2) to control their passions. Sometimes, as I think about what you and the rest of the youth of the Church are going through, I wonder if, when my own children become teenagers, they will be able to withstand the onslaught of peer pressure and control the passions that might destroy their dreams.

At times my wife and I have caught glimpses of what we hope will become our children's future. As we were leaving to go to church the other day, my little six-year-old boy, Mckay, noticed a teenage girl who, because of the way she was dressed, didn't look like she was planning to attend church.

He asked her, "What are you doing?"

"Oh, I thought I would just play with some of my friends."

I could see the wheels churning in his little mind. Then he said, "You go tell your mom not to let you play out here on Sunday. Sunday is family day."

I smiled, and thought to myself proudly, "That's my boy."

However, not long after that, he succumbed to peer pressure, and participated with four of his friends in putting one of the neighborhood cats in the freezer. After confessing what he had done, Mckay spent the afternoon in his room thinking about how he might have handled the situation differently. You see, he loves animals, and is normally very sensitive concerning them.

A few weeks later, we were grateful when he stood up against peer pressure, and did the right thing. One of his friends had a lighter and proposed using it to burn an earthworm. Mckay jumped in, grabbed the worm, and, holding it up in the air, declared, "You're not going to burn this worm! This worm is one of God's creations! It has a mom and a dad!" Then, having rescued it, he let it go.

We are a little nervous, though, about how he might control his passions when he gets to be a teenager. We recently hosted an elders quorum presidency social at our house. Everyone brought their kids, and after a while we noticed that Mckay and a little girl his age, named Sarah, were missing. We found them in a corner behind some plants, where they were kissing!

Then, the other day, he announced to me, "Dad, I've decided to get married."

I smiled and said, "Oh, really?"

"Yup!" he confirmed. "I've decided to marry Jessie (another little girl his age), in the temple."

Can you imagine the newspaper headlines: "MORMONS NOW SEALING CHILDREN TOGETHER IN TEMPLES!"?

Actually, Mckay's desire to be married in the temple is probably a wonderful consequence of the love he has for his mother, and she for him. We have observed evidence in the way Mckay thinks and acts that all of us arrive in mortality with a natural and intense need to love and to be loved. To provide for that need, Heavenly Father has equipped each of us with love buckets or hearts in which we store love and out of which we dispense love.

The gospel teaches us that *Real Love + Real Relationships* results in *Real Happiness*. Unfortunately, the world has succeeded in convincing some of us that we can find happiness in counterfeit love and counterfeit relationships. I had a difficult high school experience that taught me to be cautious in matters of love.

You know how guys, especially in high school, are motivated by food. They act like massive, endless, garbage dumps — consuming great quantities of anything edible. My high school friends and I were no different. We were good kids, but we would do just about any crazy thing for food. I recall one of my friends stalling his car for fifteen minutes in the middle of a busy intersection because he was promised food if he would dare do it. If we wanted to get someone to ask a girl out, or go and talk with someone they had never met, one of us would say, "I'll give you a hamburger if you'll do it." Someone else would say, "I'll give you an order of fries." Still another would say, "I'll give you a pie or a soft drink." It usually wouldn't take very long for us to make up our minds. "Did you say 'food'? — I'll do it!"

One night, we all went to a stake dance. The youth of our ward and our stake were very close and I believe we occasionally experienced Zion-like feelings — you know, we "were of one heart and one mind" and we usually "dwelt in righteousness" (Moses 7:18).

But, on this particular night, I let my friends push me into making a critical mistake. We were all dancing, laughing, and having a good time when one of my friends dared me to go and slow dance with a girl who we were insensitive enough to think was sort of beneath us. I'll call her Sherrie. She was self-conscious because of her appearance and very shy. If she had thought someone was going to ask her to dance on a dare, she would have been terribly hurt.

At first I said, "No way," but then someone offered me a hamburger if I would do it. Someone else offered me a pie. Others offered me fries and a soft drink. I realized that she probably hadn't danced much that night, and in the heat of the moment, I gave in to the peer pressure.

Now, there is obviously nothing wrong with asking someone to dance, but my motivation was all wrong. I wasn't thinking about her — I was thinking about the dare and the food. Besides, though she wouldn't know it, all my friends would be watching and grinning, which would be a form of ridicule. I knew it was wrong.

I wish you could have seen the look on Sherrie's face when I walked over and asked her to dance with me. She first looked surprised, and then she got a look on her face that I wasn't smart enough to fully interpret. What it said was, "Thank you for noticing me. I have been here all night hoping someone would invite me to dance. I really do want to fit in at church. I just don't quite know how." We had a nice conversation during our dance and when it was over, I walked her back to where she had been standing. Then I strutted across the stake center gym floor to my friends. Just before I reached them, I raised my hands about shoulder height and exclaimed, "I'm rich!" meaning that they owed me the food they had promised. However, just as I made my statement, the disc jockey turned down the music to make an announcement, and everyone around me, including Sherrie, heard me exclaim, "I'm rich!" I was embarrassed to think she might understand I had only danced with her on a dare. And I felt guilty.

When I told my mom what I had done she just about disowned me. From then on I never quit trying to be Sherrie's friend on the occasions when she would come to church. But little by little her problems, which I had probably added to, began to get the best of her. And in her junior year of high school a guy came along who said something like this: "I will love you, Sherrie, if you'll let me . . . " You know what I mean. Sherrie became pregnant that year and later had twins, and what had happened to her ripped me apart inside. I had had a chance to make a difference in her life and I had only added to her problems. Two years later she had another child out of wedlock, and again, it tore me apart inside.

But the story doesn't end there. One night after Sherrie and her friends had been drinking, they jumped into her pickup truck and drove down by railroad avenue in our hometown. Sherrie's reaction time must have been hampered by her drinking and it isn't really known whether or not they were trying to beat the train across the tracks, but they were hit full on by the train. It demolished the pickup truck as well as Sherrie's body. She went into a coma and the next morning her home teachers arrived at the hospital to give her a blessing. The blessing was similar to a blessing given by Alma the elder to his wayward son, Alma, many years ago. Do you remember Alma's experience while he was in *his* coma: "And it came to pass that as I was thus racked with torment, while I was harrowed up by the memory of my many sins, behold, I remembered also to have heard my father prophesy unto the people concerning the coming of one Jesus Christ, a Son of God, to atone for the sins of the world. Now, as my mind caught hold upon this thought, I cried within my heart: O Jesus, thou Son of God, have mercy on me, who am in the gall of bitterness, and am encircled about by the everlasting chains of death. And now, behold, when I thought this, I could remember my pains no more; yea, I was harrowed up by the memory of my sins no more. And oh, what joy, and what marvelous light I did behold; yea, my soul was filled with joy as exceeding as was my pain!" (Alma 36:17–20).

During the blessing, Sherrie was told that she was now going through an experience where she would have to make some choices concerning God and her life, and that her decisions would determine whether she would live or die. Well, we know about one choice she made because she lived. But the effects of the accident and the coma caused her to forget many things and to revert back to a junior high school mentality.

Over the years, I have wondered over and over in my mind: Why did I take the dare at the dance that night? Why did Sherrie take the dares and the paths she did? Why? Why?

I wonder if you might ever have felt the same way about the dares and snares you have been caught in? What were your rewards? Like the hamburger, fries, pie, soft drink, and imagined social high I thought were important, the rewards for the dares you have taken have most likely not been enduring either. Maybe you have discovered, as I have, that whatever fleeting pleasures we obtained from these kinds of activities, were not worth it. Were they?

A couple of years ago, a student and good friend of mine stood in front of his seminary class and said, "I have learned that there are two kinds of people in this world—builders and destroyers." He went on to say, "Jesus Christ was a builder, and I want to be a builder too." Then he dared the class members to be builders and not destroyers.

I later realized that there are not only dares that destroy, like with Sherrie, but there are also dares that build. Since my heart-wrenching experience with Sherrie, the words to this familiar song have meant more to me:

Dare to do right! Dare to be true!
You have a work that no other can do; . . .
Stand by your conscience, your honor, your faith; Stand like a hero
and battle till death.
Dare, dare, dare to do right;
Dare, dare, dare to be true,
Dare to be true, dare to be true.
(*Children's Songbook*, p. 158).

It was during high school that I decided I would dare to be a builder, to be true, and to do a work that no other can do. Today, I issue you this same dare. I dare you to be a builder, not a destroyer, because *you* have a work that no other can do — to build and lift the souls of others with love.

You recall the words of the Savior concerning builders and destroyers: "Beware of false prophets, who come to you in sheep's clothing, but inwardly they are ravening wolves" (3 Nephi 14:15). There are those that lie in wait to deceive and to destroy you. But sometimes it isn't easy to tell who is trying to destroy us. How can we tell? The Savior said, "Even so every good tree bringeth forth good fruit; but a corrupt tree bringeth forth evil fruit. . . . Wherefore, by their fruits ye shall know them" (3 Nephi 14:17, 20). What was Jesus saying? You can distinguish builders from destroyers by their fruits, by their works, by the consequences of their works.

After speaking at EFY in Boise, Idaho, I spent two hours talking with a girl who reminded me a great deal of Sherrie. She told me of her struggle to fit in with the LDS crowd, and described how her current alcohol- and drug-using friends had accepted her so readily. As we talked, I asked her if she was associating with builders or destroyers. She responded by saying, "My friends aren't bad people. It is just some of the things they do."

I recalled a story from the newspaper and shared it with her. It was about a sixteen-year-old boy named Mack, who, while trying to remove grass that was clogging a cornpicker, caught his left foot and right hand in the machine. In the awful fear of his predicament, he realized that if he were to save his life, he would literally have to tear his hand and foot off. It is almost impossible to comprehend how he managed to do so, but he did. And then, incredibly, he drove himself to the hospital for treatment.

It doesn't seem enough to say this experience must have been very painful, but he apparently knew what he had to do in order to save his life, and he summoned the courage to do it.

Likewise, pulling ourselves out of potentially devastating social, emotional, and spiritual situations, and terminating destructive relationships, can sometimes be similarly painful to our hearts and souls. But if we are to save our spiritual lives, we must have the courage to pull away where it is required. Ask yourself again, are you associating with builders or destroyers?

At the same time we are being careful not to permit the destroyers to weaken our faith, we must actively seek to build up others. Here are three things to consider if we are to be useful to our brothers and sisters in strengthening them:

DARE TO BE AWARE

There are too many Sherries and people like her in our lives who stand at critical crossroads and still go unnoticed. All they desire is a little bit of our attention. DARE to make yourself aware of who they are. DARE to smile and say "Hi," to sit by them, to give them your attention, to include them in your circle of friends. DARE to listen to them. To *really* listen isn't easy. Listening in this way is called having empathy, and when we have it we listen with our hearts and actually *feel* the emotions of the person who is talking to us.

Let me tell you about a girl I'll call Nancy. She gave me a shocking answer to a question I posed to my class. "If there was anything you could change about yourself, what would it be?" Her answer brought me to tears: "I wish," she wrote, "I had never been born!"

She was obviously suffering from severe depression and was even suicidal. I had spoken with her parents and they told me she had been in counseling, but that nothing seemed to work. That is, until Annalee came along. Annalee was Susan's age and they went to school together. Recognizing Susan had some problems, Annalee took an interest in her. She made it a point to walk her to class, to sit by her, to call her on the phone, and to even go to Susan's house to visit. Over a two-month period, I saw a miracle occur as Susan found she had a true friend who loved her in spite of her problems. I'll never forget the day Susan looked me right in the eye, gave me a vigorous handshake, and with a smile said, "Hi, Brother Harris. How are you doing?" For most people that would be a normal thing to do—for Susan, it was a major breakthrough. Thank goodness for people like Annalee, and like you, who care enough to be aware of others.

DARE TO SHARE

Our time and talents are precious commodities not easily shared with others. The Sherries in our lives need to know that they are worth the sharing of our time and talents with them. Sometimes my little boy will come running in and say, "Dad, let's wrestle." He just needs to know I care and that I'm willing to share my time with him. (The other day I taught him a new wrestling move and he pinned my wife. It was great.)

I'll never forget the day a severely handicapped girl stood up in my class and said, "Iii neeeed a ffrriend tooo ssiitt byy meee att llunch." She then waited to see who would respond. Finally, Treasure and Wendy said they would sit by her every day. They not only sat by her, they walked her to class, and had her over to watch videos of her favorite singer, Barry Manilow. As people began to understand what a beautiful person there was inside, they too became willing to share their time and talents with her. She was even elected to be an attendant at one of the school dances. After watching her daughter struggle across the stage to receive her diploma at seminary graduation, her mom wept as she tried to express her thanks for the many people who had befriended her.

DARE TO BEWARE

You could be the next casualty just like Sherrie. Most sin happens because of the two toughest challenges for teenagers. Remember, (1) to stand up to peers, and (2) to control your passions. Why take the first drink? Why experiment with the first fix? It usually happens because of peer pressure — someone dares you to do it. It can happen to anyone and it always destroys lives. For example, a number of months ago, a very close friend of our family was found in one of the back streets of San Francisco with a blood-alcohol level of .586. A level of .600 is lethal. She never thought just one drink would lead to the breakup of her marriage, the loss of her two boys, and a life of living on the streets.

Have you ever wondered why there is so much immorality in the world? One reason is that human passions are strong and insistent. It takes determination to resist them, and wise young people will take care not to put themselves in a situation where they are likely to be tempted. Perhaps you have heard it said that the last best friend you date is the best friend you marry. Be careful, because immorality can destroy your dreams and it can happen to anyone. I remember hearing a regional representative years ago who said, "I don't care who you are. I don't care if you are an apostle in the Church. If you put yourselves in potentially compromising situations enough, you WILL fall." It is the Lord's intention and the purpose of his church to help us resist temptation and to keep ourselves morally clean.

So what will it be? Hamburgers, fries, pies, and a soft drink or some other fleeting momentary pleasure, which will drain and starve you and those around you of love? Or will you *Dare* to do right, *Dare* to be true, *Dare* to be a builder, and *Dare* to do a work that no other can do? I believe you will take the Dare to be Aware, the Dare to Share, and the Dare to Beware. There is so much we can do to lift and strengthen others. I bear you my humble witness that this gospel and Church are true, that Jesus is the

Christ, and that by following him we can obtain greater happiness, richness, and depth in our everyday lives. May the Lord bless you. The Sherries and other people in your lives are counting on you!

Victor Harris teaches seminary at Logan High School. He earned his bachelor's degree in psychology at Brigham Young University and is working on a master's degree in marriage and family relations. Brother Harris enjoys all sports (particularly tennis, basketball, and wrestling) and is also a singer and an entertainer, having performed with The Young Ambassadors and U.S.O. groups. Victor and his wife, Heidi, have three children.

10

STAND AS A WITNESS

CURTIS JACOBS

During the persecutions suffered by the Latter-day Saints in Missouri, Benjamin F. Johnson endured a terrifying experience. He'd been taken prisoner by a hostile group of men commanded by General Clark. While sitting on a log, Benjamin was confronted by a man with a rifle, who demanded that he "give up Mormonism right now, or I'll shoot you." Benjamin refused. Then taking deliberate aim at the defenseless Mormon, the ruffian pulled the trigger of his rifle. Nothing happened. The man then uttered a few non-celestial words, told the world how he'd used this gun for twenty years without it ever misfiring, examined the lock, put fresh powder in it, aimed it at Benjamin, and pulled the trigger. Again, nothing happened. A few non-terrestrial words were hurled through the air, and once again the gun was checked and reloaded. When the blasphemer pulled the trigger this time, the gun exploded, killing the would-be assassin right there and then. (E. Dale Le Baron, "Benjamin F. Johnson: Colonizer, Public Servant, and Church Leader," Master's Thesis, Brigham Young University, pp. 42–43). Three strikes and you're out!

Most of us will probably never have to stand up for the Church or our beliefs in quite the same way as Benjamin Johnson (thank goodness), yet all who have entered into the baptismal covenant have promised to stand as witnesses. Every week, all over the world, young women of the Church recite, "We are daughters of our Heavenly Father who loves us, and we love Him. *We will stand as witnesses of God at all times, in all things, and in all places.*"

What does it really mean, to "stand as witnesses"? The word *stand* has many definitions, but "to take or maintain a (specified) position, to resist, to endure" seem to apply. The word *witness* simply means to "serve as evidence of" someone, or something. Therefore, we are to take a specific position, and act as disciples of the Lord.

As the Young Women's theme suggests, there are three conditions in which we pledge to "stand as witnesses":

FIRST: "AT ALL TIMES"

Always? Really? Yes. We all probably know someone who is really good on Sundays, but who misbehaves on Friday or Saturday nights. Right? A couple of years after I started teaching seminary in Arizona, I couldn't make it to a football game to watch our "mighty" McClintock Chargers play. My wife was willing to go for me, and bring me a report of the game. Not many of my students knew who she was, but she knew many of them, so she sat and watched—not only the game, but my students. Most of them were "screaming their heads off," which is generally the way we behave at football games. My wife took special notice of one LDS girl who was yelling encouragement like everyone else, except she was using language totally unlike her "Sunday vernacular." In fact, she was employing profanity to emphasize her feelings. Sitting as she was, surrounded by many nonmember friends, she certainly didn't provide a very good example of the Church. I've often wondered what they thought of her—and of us.

On the other hand, many LDS youth realize the importance of standing as witnesses at all times. At a certain high school in Idaho, there was a popular annual tradition just prior to graduation. The senior class boys would attend a great big "kegger" party. Those who wanted to attend had to pay $5.00, in advance. The time and place was never announced until a day or two before, to prevent parents or school officials from interfering.

One concerned young lady stood up in her seminary class and brought up the subject of the beer party. She said that her boy friend, who had "never had a drink before," was planning to attend the "kegger." She was unhappy about his decision, and appealed to the class for help in persuading him not to go.

The teacher asked, "Well? What can we do?" There was a lot of talk, but nobody seemed to have an idea about what could be done, that is, until the next day. Two young men from the class showed up at the seminary teacher's door with a plan. One of them had a friend whose father owned a grocery store, and who was willing to supply all the fried chicken and soft drinks that could be consumed at a "good guys" party — the charge would only be $1.50 per person, payable in advance.

The day came that the time and place of the "kegger party" was being whispered around. That same day, the "good guys" party was announced over the p.a. system at school. "Ironically," it was to be held at the same time as the beer party. Suddenly, people started asking for their money back from the planners of the "kegger." They wanted to go to the "good guys" party instead.

The night of the parties came, and at about 11:00 P.M. the seminary teacher heard something banging on his window. He looked out and heard someone shout, "He's awake!" He went downstairs (partly because of the loud noise that was being caused by the many fists pounding on his front door), and opened the door to find forty to fifty happy young men singing, "We Thank Thee, O God, for a Prophet." Several in the group were fellows who had previously planned to be at the "kegger." He later found out that only two young men (the organizers) showed up for the beer party, and they got bored, and finally gave it up, saying, "(H——, this ain't no fun."

Two young men stood as witnesses and made a real difference in the lives of many more.

SECOND: "IN ALL THINGS"

At one time I was teaching seminary by a high school in Arizona where only about 5 percent of the students were LDS.

Even though few in number, the Mormons were all known by their religion to the other students. Some of my students were embarrassed to openly come to seminary. To avoid being seen, they would cross the street first, then walk behind a business complex to the back of the seminary building. Some were less inhibited about their religion. For instance, one young man took a dare to go outside the seminary building and yell at the top of his lungs, "I'm a Mormon, and I'm proud of it!" As he did so, the rest of the class ran as fast as they could to hide in the building.

However, there were other evidences of courage and pride in speaking up for the Church. Each student in the high school was permitted to write a little statement or description to be printed in the yearbook, next to his or her picture. Several of the Mormon kids mentioned the Church, and one of them boldly wrote, "Nephi is a radical dude. Read the Book of Mormon."

One young man I taught seemed to have it all—good looks, a terrific personality, outstanding athletic talent, popularity, and a great family. He played on the school basketball team, and was as straight as they come. There was another young man in the school who was totally the opposite. Abused as a boy, he was unloved, uncared for, an extremely slow learner, and he had little athletic talent. He had few if any friends, and was considered by nearly everyone to be a complete "zero."

Well, my good-looking young man, we'll call him Sean, decided to take this kid under his wing. Sean took him around with him, picked him up for school activities, introduced him to people, defended him, and most important, became his friend. One evening my wife and I went to a movie, and there were Sean and his date, *and* this young man. The feeling around school was that since he was Sean's friend, you'd better be nice to him.

During his senior year, Sean was nominated for homecoming king. There were five other guys (none of whom were members of the Church) running. Well, Sean won. But not only did he win, he got more votes than the other five combined. The announcement that Sean had been elected "King" of homecoming was made during halftime at the football game. It was also announced that two young ladies had received the same number of votes, and so there would be two "Queens" that year—something that had never happened before. (You can imagine what went through the minds of people when they realized that a "Mormon" had been given two "queens." Oh, well.) Whether in school, on the court, with friends, with young ladies, or befriending the unloved, Sean stood as a witness "in all things."

THIRD: "IN ALL PLACES"

Several years ago a young LDS woman was attending the University of Utah. After class one day, a young man approached her, and asked her out on a date. They made arrangements and the night of the date came. He picked her up, took her on the date, and afterward proceeded to do what *he* was used to doing. He drove up the canyon, stopped the car, and started putting the moves on this young lady. She quickly stopped him with, "I don't do that kind of thing." He couldn't believe it. Oh, he thought, she is probably just playing hard to get, right? After a few minutes he began to try again. This time, she stopped him with, "You must be deaf. I don't do that!" Like Joseph fled when Potiphar's wife put the moves on him, this wonderful young woman got out of the car and began walking home.

The young man moved away to another state. Years later some missionaries happened to knock on his door. He opened the door slightly, just far enough for him to see who was there, and them slammed it shut. The elders had just long enough to see that the interior of the house was a total wreck.

"Just a minute," a voice called out through the door.

They stood on the doorstep, listening to what sounded like a great commotion—things being banged around. After a few moments, the door opened again, but this time things were different. The place was a lot neater and cleaner, and they were asked to come in. They were invited to sit down, and the young man who answered the door asked if they were Mormons.

"Yes," they were.

He then proceeded to tell them about the Mormon girl back in Utah whom he had taken to the canyon. He asked, "What is it about your church that would prompt her to do what she did?"

The missionaries began to teach this young man, and you can guess what happened. Within a couple of weeks he had changed his habits, prepared himself, and was ready to enter the waters of baptism.

Now, may I ask you a question? What if the young woman hadn't said no? Do you think this young man would be a member of the Church today? Her willingness to stand as a witness had a great effect, and she didn't even know about it. Her story bears out Elder Neal A. Maxwell's advice to youth: "Be different from the world in order to make a difference in the world." ("These Are Your Days," *New Era,* January–February 1985, p. 6.)

Have you ever considered that before we were born, we may have made covenants and promises to do certain things? Referring in part to something taught by Orson Hyde, Elder Maxwell said of the premortal world: "We understood things better there than we do in this lower world. He [Elder Hyde] surmised as to the agreements we made there that 'it is not impossible that we signed the articles thereof with our own hands'. . . *our forgetfulness cannot alter the facts.*" ("A More Determined Discipleship," *Ensign,* February, 1979, p. 72; italics added.)

How are you doing in regard to keeping your premortal promises? Do you realize there may well be people who are counting on you?

Not too long ago, I heard a young woman bear her testimony. She told about her brother, who had called her on the telephone, ecstatic because he had picked up a fumble in a football game, and had run for a touchdown. There had been only one opponent in a position to stop him, but a halfback teammate had blocked the defender, making it possible for him to score the touchdown that made him so excited.

A couple of days later the entire team was invited to a "party." The fellow who scored the touchdown took his halfback buddy with him — the one who had made it possible for him to score the touchdown. Arriving at the party, he could see there was some drinking going on, and decided to leave. He regretted not insisting his friend (the halfback) leave with him, particularly when he learned the next day that his friend had gotten drunk and crashed on his motorcycle. He was in the hospital, in a coma. The young man chastised himself, saying, "He was there for me, why wasn't I there for him?"

I have a letter from a young man who had a contrasting experience while serving on his mission. He said:

> We were out knocking on doors. . . . It was about 11:30 so I told my comp [that's mission jargon for companion] that we would knock this one last street, and then go to lunch. We got in the first house and taught a lengthy discussion. By then it was about 12:30, so rather than knocking the rest of the street, we just went to lunch. About halfway through lunch a little lady, about sixty years old, showed up at the dining hall. . . . She asked for the two nice young men in white shirts and ties, and was directed to the back room where we were eating. She approached us and as we shook hands, she looked sorrowfully into my eyes, and sobbingly asked why we hadn't stopped at her house that morning. She told us that she had been waiting to see us, and begged us to please come back in two days because she needed to tell us something important. As she left, she kissed my hand and thanked me.
>
> We did call on her. She was excited and hurried to find two broken chairs for us to sit on. She started to cry, and as the tears fell, she told us about a dream that she had had over twenty years before. She explained that at the time she had the dream she had lost everything — her mother, her husband, her fortune, — everything she owned. She was totally devastated. The only thing she had left was her faith in God, and that was quickly diminishing. She finally reached her last straw.
>
> That night before going to bed she knelt down and pleaded with Heavenly Father not to abandon her. That night as she slept, she dreamed she went to heaven and saw there a young man wearing a white, long-sleeved shirt. He was kind of blond and radiated a strong feeling of love. She went to him, and dropping to his feet, began pleading with him to help her find her way. He bent down, and lifting her to her feet, told her to be patient, that he was coming to help her. He comforted her with a hug and left. She ran after him, and again begged him for help. He looked very deeply and lovingly into her eyes and said, "Just wait for me, I'm coming."
>
> For twenty years she had been waiting and watching for

that young man. Well, three weeks ago she was in the city and saw him. She hurried as fast as she could, but the bus left before she got there. She noted that the bus was going to the city where she lived. She prayed constantly that God would send that young man to her. Then she saw him again. He was across the street at her neighbor's house. Hoping he would come to her house, she waited and waited. When he failed to do so, she asked her neighbor who those young men had been, and learned they were Mormon missionaries. She finally found us in the dining hall. As you have probably already guessed, I am the young man from her dream.

How grateful he must be that he was willing to stand as a witness and serve the Lord.

You have so much to offer the world. Be the best you can be. Be grateful for the gospel, for your life, for the truths that are yours, and most of all, for the Savior. Be determined to stand as a witness of God at all times, in all things, and in all places.

Curtis L. Jacobs is an institute of religion instructor at Utah State University. Holding a master's degree in counseling and guidance, he has taught both seminary and institute in Arizona. Curtis enjoys playing racquetball, and he held a championship in the sport while residing in Prescott, Arizona. His other interests include basketball, piano, old movies, and Les Miserables. *He and his wife, Jolene, have three children.*

11

I JUST WANT TO BE HAPPY

BARBARA BARRINGTON JONES

Recently I received a letter from a young woman in which she said, "I would like to ask you something if I could. I know you're not a counselor or anything, but I was wondering how I could feel better about myself, feel more accepted by my peers, and be more happy all the time." She went on to say, "I dread getting up every morning to go to school. My sister and I have not been getting along either. She's seventeen, and I'm sixteen. She has a boyfriend and is very pretty. She's skinny and used to be a model. I'm nothing like that. So I think I'm a little jealous."

Before I tell you how I answered her letter, let's back up a little bit and talk about feeling good about ourselves.

When we're born, we have 100 percent self-esteem. Considering where we just came from, why would we have any less? Then things start to change. By the time we get into grade school, here are the statistics:

67 percent of the guys still feel good about themselves;

60 percent of the girls feel positive about themselves.

In high school, 49 percent of the boys feel good about themselves. That means over half don't feel good about themselves.

And just 24 percent of the girls feel good. (Statistics provided by *The American Association of University Women.*)

Why?

Why do we lose our self-esteem? Why do we lose our capacity to be happy? Why do we become blind to our real potential?

My husband cut an article out of "Dear Abby" for me. The

headline was "Don't Judge a Gift by Its Cover." The letter told this story:

A young man from a wealthy family was about to graduate from high school. It was the custom in that affluent neighborhood for the parents to give the graduate an automobile. "Bill" and his father had spent months looking at cars, and the week before graduation they found the perfect car. Bill was certain the car would be his on graduation night.

Imagine his disappointment when, on the eve of his graduation, Bill's father handed him a gift wrapped Bible! Bill was so angry that he threw the Bible down and stormed out of the house. He and his father never saw each other again. It was the news of his father's death that finally brought Bill home.

As he sat one night going through his father's possessions that he was to inherit, he came across the Bible his father had given him. He brushed away the dust and opened it to find a cashier's check, dated the day of his graduation, in the exact amount of the price of the car they had chosen together.

As you read this, I believe your reaction will be much like mine. I said to myself, "Stupid, stupid guy. Why didn't you just open your gift? Didn't you know that in this book there is everything you could ever want? Not only would you have had the material thing you wanted — the car — but you would have had an instruction manual on how to live this life and how to be happy." He was too quick to judge the gift that was given him.

What can we learn from this story?

We came to earth with everything: 100 percent self-esteem and countless gifts from Heavenly Father. But we have to search for our gifts. We have to open each gift and make the most of it. We all have gifts, but what makes me so sad is that so many times we don't recognize them, because we spend so much time comparing ourselves to others.

This is a portion of a letter I received from a girl. She wrote:

I feel so inadequate, so inferior, so average. I watch and study everyone around me — people, pictures in magazines, actresses, everyone — picking out every feature that I wish I could have for myself. In every person I see a trait that I rip myself apart for not having or for not being able to do as well. Jealousy has made me a depressed and hopeless person.

I'll go through everything, one thing at a time. I'm overweight and have been forever. Furthermore, I make goals continually and fail every time. I am absolutely totally grotesque.

My hair's a mess — permed, colored, no shine. It's not romantically long, or curly, or short, or stylish — it's nothing.

My eyebrows are each different. They have no shape or curved line. They droop and the hair grows in all directions.

My eyelashes grow every direction and cannot be straightened or curled. They are also not long, dark, curly, or full.

My nose is long, even my mother would admit, because she has the same one, only not quite as bad.

My face is round and chubby. My skin is splotched. My teeth are straight, but very yellowish in color because of another one of my revolting self-destructive, spiritually killing, socially repulsive, habits — bulimia.

She went on to list every part of herself she disliked, right down to her toes. Do you see what she's doing? Every day she's looking in that mirror and picking herself apart. It is not constructive criticism. She's destroying herself by overlooking the good things about herself. But this isn't going on just with young women.

I met a young man in Dallas at a youth conference. His parents later flew him to my house to go through my seminar because his self-esteem was so low. His name is Paul Anderson.

When I first met him, he was slim, not too tall, and couldn't look you in the face. In trying to get to know him, I asked, "What do you like to do? Do you like to play sports?"

He said, "No, I hate sports."

"How about school? Do you like school?"

"No, not really."

My husband and I spent one solid week trying to get him to say something he liked to do, trying to get him to open the cover and take his gift out of the box. He wouldn't do it.

Finally, at the end of the week, I asked him, "What do you do when you get home from school?"

He said, "Play the piano."

"Oh, you play the piano?"

"Yeah. Do you want to see pictures of my family?"

The first picture he pulled out of his wallet was of his brother — a total jock — captain of the football team, blond crew cut, and a muscular build.

What had my friend been doing? He had been comparing himself with his brother. He acted as if his piano playing were unimportant or insignificant.

I asked, "What kind of things do you play on the piano after school?"

He went into my living room, sat down at the piano, and, with an attitude of who cares anyway? said, "Well, I wrote this."

He stared playing this beautiful piece of music that he had composed.

I couldn't believe it. He was totally ignoring his own gifts because he was so busy judging himself by the outside — the cover. And his cover wasn't like his brother's.

He worked on overcoming his negative attitude about himself. He eventually served a mission, then, after he returned, he sent me the cover of his first album. With a great-looking photo of himself on the front, it was entitled, "Paul Anderson, Himself." He had written: "To Sister Jones, who has given me so much. I love you tons. Paul." He had unwrapped his gift and made it available for the whole world to enjoy.

All he had to do was open the gift.

Do you base how you feel on how you perform? Do you base how you feel about yourself on what other people say? Do you base how you feel about yourself on your physical appearance?

You have so many gifts that are untouched. But you have to do your part. Heavenly Father is not going to do it for you. You have to take the gift out. You have to search for it. God judges from the inside.

The greatest thing that you can do for your self-esteem is to come to know the Savior. As I was teaching a class the other day, a bishop walked up to the front of the room, right in the middle of the class. He asked, "May I say something?"

I handed the microphone to him. This is the story he told:

When I was eight years old, I was really into baseball. I had every player's baseball card. My dad saved his money to send me to a baseball camp run by a star player.

The first day, the famous guy running the camp, who was kind of cocky, had the list of names. My name is spelled S-t-e-p-h-e-n. He looked at the list and asked, "Where's old Step-han?" He purposely mispronounced my name.

I cringed as everyone started to laugh.

The coach continued to call, "Step-han, are you here? Hey, Step-han."

I felt worse and worse. Everyone was laughing harder and harder. It was the worst experience of my life. When I got home, I told my dad I would never play baseball again.

My dad was a wise man and waited a few years. Then a retired player came to town and started a Little League program. Dad took the new coach aside and said, "My son loves baseball so much. But he had a bad experience with a coach." And he told the coach the whole story.

The new coach said, "You send him to me for tryouts."

I barely made the team, but improved as the season progressed. Then the time came when it was a win or lose situation for my team. The bases were loaded. It was my turn at bat. I thought the coach was going to bring in a pinch hitter for me. But the coach didn't. He walked over and put his arm around me and said, "Stephen, you can do it. I'm your coach. I'm behind you all the way. You can do it."

I walked up to the plate. I did not hit the ball out of the ballpark. But I did hit a fly to the centerfielder that was deep enough to allow the runner from third to tag up and beat the throw to home. Our team won the game.

Stephen's coach had faith in him.

The bishop continued his story:

I'll never forget that coach. Then I grew up and got another coach in my life. My new coach came to me one night and said, Stephen, "you're going on a mission." And when I said to him, "I don't think

I can do it," he said, "I have faith in you. I know you can do it."
My new coach was Jesus Christ.

I went on a mission. Then my coach came to me again one
night, after I had gotten married, and said, "Stephen, you're going
to be in charge of the Blazer Bs."

I said, "Coach, I can't be in charge of them."

The Savior said, "Yes, you can. I have faith in you."

And then this newly called, young bishop, with emotion chok-
ing him, said, "He came to me two months ago and said, 'Stephen,
you're going to be the bishop.'"

And Stephen said, "I can't be the bishop."

The Savior said, "I'll be right beside you every step of the
way."

This man learned to listen to the one who knew his potential
and who would support him.

The only way you'll be happy, the only way you'll feel good
about yourself, is to get a new *coach*. Listen to someone who
knows and loves the real you. Make the Savior Jesus Christ your
coach.

That's the most important piece of advice I can give you.

I would like to close with a true story about an immigrant
girl who, at the age of fifteen, just ached inside because she was
so unhappy. Coming from a foreign country, she felt that she
would never be accepted, or ever have friends. During the two
years she had been attending high school since arriving in the
United States from Germany, she had seldom spoken to any of
the other students. She never felt like she fit in. She was self-
conscious about her accent, her hand-me-down clothes, her long,
thick braids, and even her lunches of dark rye bread that her
mother packed for her each day.

One day as she sat in the library reading a book, she looked
outside the window at two girls who were sitting on the lawn.
They were laughing and talking together. She could tell they were
best friends. "Oh, I just wish I could have a friend, even one
friend, that I could talk with," she thought.

When she got home, she went to her room, sat on the edge
of her bed, put her face in her hands, and cried. As the tears

streamed down her cheeks, she lifted her head, and her gaze fell
on a picture of the Savior, hanging on the wall across the room.
She thought how friendly his face looked. She had been taught
all her life how much he loves and cares for each of us. As she
looked at the picture, she whispered, "Jesus, I'm so lonely."

The next day after school one of the girls asked her if she
would be going to the school dance that night. She abruptly said,
"No!" As she boarded the bus to go home, all she could think of
was the last dance she had attended, where she had sat on the
sidelines for hours by herself. Finally, a young man had walked
up to her, but instead of asking her to dance, he had yanked on
one of her braids. Everyone had laughed, and she had been humiliated. No, she would never go to a dance again.

Reaching home, she walked through the stillness of her empty
house. Her mother worked every day, and her younger sisters
and brother were out playing with their friends. If they had friends,
why couldn't she have friends? Was there something wrong with
her? She ran to her room and threw herself on the bed. Her body
shook with sobs.

She sat up suddenly. Someone was in the room! Quickly, she
wiped away her tears so that whoever it was wouldn't know she
had been crying. She looked around, but saw no one there. There
was an undeniable presence and a feeling of overwhelming love
like she had never felt before. She knew who it was. "Jesus,"
she whispered, "is it you?"

He answered, not with a voice that could be heard by human
ears, but with a feeling of love so strong that it penetrated her
heart. She saw no human form, but with her spirit she saw his
smiling face, and his eyes that seemed to say, "You are my special
friend." And, sitting there on her bed, she seemed to hear his
gentle words, "I will never leave you or forsake you. Don't be
afraid or ashamed. I love you just the way you are." She had never
felt such unconditional love in her life.

For three glorious months that presence stayed with her. He
was there when she awoke, and when she caught the bus. He
stood by her desk in school, and ran beside her in gym. She was

gloriously happy. Her family couldn't believe it as they observed her smiling and heard her humming as she set the table.

One day at the bus stop, as the usual group of teens gathered, he seemed to say to her, "Aren't these youth great? I love each one of them dearly." She smiled as she began to see her class-mates through the Savior's eyes. It wasn't long before they began to include her in their conversations. At last, she was beginning to belong. At last, she felt accepted. At last, she was happy.

She awoke one morning to find the presence gone. She won-dered if she had done something wrong. She confessed every sin, but she was still alone. In desperation, she picked up her Bible looking for those special words that he had said to her that first day. She found them in Hebrews 13:5, "For he hath said, I will never leave thee, nor forsake thee."

He said, "never," so that she might know that even though she didn't feel his presence, he was still with her. She seemed to hear him say, "You will find me in my written word, and in the faces of the people you meet, and in many other different ways." She suddenly realized how blessed she had been to have the Savior with her for that very special time in her life. He had taught her that true happiness comes from seeing ourselves and others through his eyes. (Adapted from Helen Grace Lescheid, *Guideposts,* September 1992.)

The Savior will be there as our special friend and our *Coach.* If we follow his perfect example to love others as he loves us, we will find true happiness.

Barbara Barrington Jones is an international image consultant, author, lecturer, fashion designer, former classical ballet dancer and actress, and professional model. A director of summer youth programs at BYU, Sister Jones also grooms young women for competition in national and international beauty pageants. She en-joys walking, preparing and eating healthy foods, and working with youth. Barbara and her husband, Hal, reside in Novato, California, and they have two children.

FANTASYLAND OR REALITYLAND: NICE PLACES TO VISIT, BUT WHERE DO YOU WANT TO LIVE?

ALLEN LITCHFIELD

Did you make childhood pledges when you were very young, about the way it would be when you were older? As a pre-schooler, I loved pickles. My mother tells me that as a boy of three or four, I swore that when I was a dad, I wouldn't put the lid on the pickles so tight that my kids couldn't get at them. When my wife was a child, she decided that big bunches of bananas would hang in her home so that her children could have a banana whenever they wanted. Later in my youth, my family visited my Uncle Wayne's home in Bountiful, Utah. We children were amazed by something in their home — they had candy dishes in various places around the house — filled with candy! My Aunt Verl said we could just help ourselves! Now I am a parent, and looking back, I can understand why my mother must have been embarrassed when my brother and I emptied every candy dish in their home, and then asked for more. But that night we both vowed to have brimming candy dishes in every room in our homes when we were adults.

I remember many nights in my childhood, after being sent off to bed, lying there thinking that I would let my children stay up as late as they wanted to. At various other times in my childhood, I declared that I would let my children: eat in front of the TV every night; have their dessert first; skip vegetables they didn't like; play before doing homework; and have breakfast cereals called Pure Sugar, and Huge-Toy-in-Every-Box Flakes. One Halloween, my sons declared that they would let their children go out "trick or treating" as late as they wanted, and then "eat the whole haul in one night, if they wished." I suppose children throughout the world make plans like these.

Disneyland opened in California in the 1950s, when I was a small boy growing up in Canada. Some of my friends went to Disneyland for holidays and brought back great stories of their adventures. On the Mickey Mouse Club television show, scenes were sometimes showed of Disneyland, filled with children giddy with pleasure. Although we never went there as children, we knew all about the Tea Cups, the Dumbo Ride, the Jungle Cruise, the Matterhorn roller-coaster, the Sky-Tram, and the center of Fantasyland—Sleeping Beauty's castle. My family went on some great vacations, mostly to places in Utah, where my grandmother lived, but we never got to Disneyland. As a young boy I covenanted that when I was a father, I would take my family and *move* to Disneyland. Childhood plans are often vague and impractical, but I thought then that there would be a way to actually live in the park. I thought we could probably camp out on Tom Sawyer Island, sleep on one of the big ships on the river, or get a nice room in the castle itself. When my older brother challenged my plans by saying that no one was allowed to sleep on the attractions, I conceded that we might have to sleep elsewhere, but could spend every day there. My children were going to Disneyland!

I am an adult now, married with six children. I don't remember to leave the pickle jar lid loose. Sometimes there isn't even a pickle or "anything good" in the refrigerator. There isn't a huge bunch of bananas hanging from the ceiling in our kitchen. We have just a few candy dishes and they are full for only a few minutes each year during the Christmas season. Our youngest children are usually sent off to bed at an early hour, often when it is still light. In our home we almost never eat in front of the TV; dessert is given to those who eat their vegetables; we often have oatmeal for breakfast; and we insist that homework be done before play. My wife and I have turned into mostly boring, responsible adults. However, one childhood promise has been kept. We do go to Disneyland!

This is not a commercial announcement like we have all seen at the end of the Super Bowl or some other sporting event, where a media person rushes up to the MVP of the game to interview him. The star of the game is holding a soft drink (that he has been paid to hold), wearing athletic gear or shoes (that he gets millions a year to endorse), and has a cap on his head that advertises some other company. The interviewer asks him what he's going to do now, and the star shouts, "I'm going to Disneyland!" He gets paid about a zillion dollars for saying this one sentence.

Now, the Disney people have not paid me a single penny to say this, but we like Disneyland! Splash Mountain, the Haunted Mansion, Pirates of the Caribbean, Flight of Peter Pan, Thunder Mountain Railroad, Star Tours, and Space Mountain are some of our favorite attractions. The Disney people have gone to great lengths to make these simulated experiences seem "real." They have created meticulously detailed sets so that Br'er Rabbit, the ghosts, the pirates, and the flights over Never-Never Land and through space come alive.

These rides and attractions are really well done. Our children never tire of their favorites, and are even willing to wait in long lines to experience them. But never have our children thought of them as "real." They have always seemed to understand that these are fantasy experiences. We have never taken any of our children under the age of five, but we have noticed that some tiny children cry and scream with fright on some of the rides. They are terrified because they cannot distinguish between real and pretend. However, it seems that at a later age, children love the adventure and get absorbed by it. They can even pretend they are flying a space ship, are on a pirate raid, or are driving a racing car. But when the ride is over, they know who they are and where they really are. Our children have enjoyed being photographed with the Disney characters and sometimes have collected their autographs. But even our youngest children have been aware that Roger Rabbit and Minnie Mouse are just people dressed up in costumes. Being able to distinguish between the real and the fantasy might be one part of the maturation process. Maturity doesn't mean we can't have fun with fantasy, it just means that we recognize it for what it is.

One time our family was about halfway through the Splash Mountain log flume ride, when some part of the machinery broke down and our log car stopped. We were ushered out of the log we had been floating in, through a door in the wall, down some steps, and out into a back lot. In just a few seconds, we left the imaginary world of Br'er Fox and Br'er Bear and found ourselves outside in the California sunshine. From the backside the fabulous ride was just a drab grey building, filled with pumps, lights, mannequins, and special effects. In some ways, it was more of a disappointment for the adults than the children to see the fantasy exposed so abruptly. But, by the end of a long day at the park, children are usually content to leave the glitzy fantasy world, clutching real parents' hands and necks, and yearning for real pillows and beds. Adults get a taste of reality immediately, as they drive out of the park and hit the traffic on the L.A. freeways.

Another theme park in southern California, Universal Studios Tour, demonstrates how fantasy worlds are created in the movies. At various places in the tour, visitors are shown how special effects are used in such film productions as *Back to the Future, Backdraft, Star Trek,* and other movies. You might leave the tour thinking that nothing in movies is real — the houses are just fronts, the punches don't really land, the ocean is a tiny pond, the shark is a fake-looking machine, the car has no engine, the blood is chocolate syrup, the space ship is just a model about the size of a loaf of bread, and so on. And yet after the tour, you still enjoy going to the movies, still get involved with the action and romance, and sometimes almost believe that the movies are real.

As a teenager, my wife saw a scary movie called *Wait Until Dark.* It was not a slasher "Jason VII vs. Candyman on Elm Street" saga. It was about a blind woman who was deceived and harassed by some gangsters. Near the end of the movie they try to kill the woman to get something she has accidently obtained. I have attempted to watch a video of the movie with my wife on a number of occasions. She is always frightened near the end and closes her eyes to shut out the terror. At the climactic point, she can't even stay in the room, because she can hear the sound track and can't stand the tension.

Now, my wife is a bright woman who did very well in college. She is rationally aware that Audrey Hepburn, the star, won't be killed because: (1) it is just a movie, (2) Hepburn survived to make other movies, and (3) we've seen the show many times and know how it ends. But my wife still can't stay in the room and watch the ending. It is just too real and scary. Fantasy, done well, *can* seem very real. In fact, fantasy is often accepted as reality by intelligent and rational people in our society. I know some young people who are aware that Sleeping Beauty and Marty McFly are imaginary characters. They know that kisses from princes won't counteract poison apples, and that driving 88 miles per hour won't take us into the future. (Some have even tried kissing while driving 88 miles per hour just to prove it.) These are rational young people who seem to know much about what is real, but many are still deceived by fantasies. They would never be fooled by the fantasy world of amusement parks. Our youth know that the ghosts in the Haunted Mansion are holograms and some can even explain in technical terms how the hologram works. Yet many of these youth are fooled by more subtle and pernicious fantasies.

Some fantasies are obvious. The most gullible and easily deceived people in the world are those who think that the fantasy world of professional wrestling is for real. These people should probably not be allowed to vote or be issued driver's licenses. When they watch an apparently hate-filled 400-pound monster named Volcano try to destroy a seven-foot-tall creature called Funeral Director, they think it quite reasonable that he push his opponent into those heavily padded turnbuckles in the corners rather than punching him right in the jaw or breaking his arm. One of the questions on the American College Test is, "Do you believe that those giant professional wrestlers are actually fighting?" Please be aware that if you mark "yes" on that question, no college in the western world will admit you.

But there are many fantasies that are more widely believed by the public than TV wrestling. For example, most of us think that those stunningly handsome and beautiful people on the covers of magazines are way better looking than everyone else. Michelle Pfeiffer was featured on the cover of *Esquire* magazine last year, about the time the movie *Batman Returns,* in which she played Catwoman, came out. The caption on her picture read, "What Michelle Pfeiffer Needs . . . Is Absolutely Nothing." But another magazine, *Harper's,* offered proof in their edition the following month that even the Beautiful People need a little help. *Harper's* had obtained the photo retoucher's bill for Pfeiffer's picture on the *Esquire* cover. The retouchers charged $1,525 to render the following services: "Clean up complexion, soften smile line, trim chin, soften line under earlobe, add hair, add forehead to create better line, and soften neck muscles." The editor of *Harper's* printed the story because we are, he said, "constantly faced with perfection in magazines; this is to remind the reader . . . there's a difference between real life and art."

This is why you shouldn't be comparing your yearbook or driver's license photographs with the magazine cover faces. The photographer who is shooting your picture is getting paid minimum wage, is bored, in a hurry, and may even hate you. Little wonder your picture comes out looking awful. I've imagined that if, by some fluke, your final photo comes out pretty well, the developers destroy the negative, and make the photographer shoot a "retake" — to insure you look really horrid. So, trying to look really nice for the yearbook photos is a waste of time and effort. It is like trying to look as mature as the "teenagers" in the movies and on television. Remember that the "high school students" in the movie *Grease* were in their late twenties and mid-thirties. Some of the stars of a television series about southern California students who have memorized their zip code, finished high school about ten years ago. One actor playing a teenager on a show about a very young doctor is twenty-eight years old. The point is that it is impossible to look like these people — so "don't worry, be happy," with the way you look — at least you are *real.*

Tall, slim models, and movie stars who spend three hours a day exercising, who spend a hundred dollars a day for special fat-free and calorie-free food, who have a team of six beauticians waiting on them hand and foot, and who have had numerous episodes of cosmetic surgery, are often our role models. The media shows us these "perfect people" and makes us feel inferior when we don't measure up. When we shop for clothes and discover we don't look quite as cool as the people in magazine advertisements for those clothes, we sometimes feel that there is something wrong with us! We must be too fat, or too skinny, or too short, or too tall. Or, we convince ourselves we are not filled out well enough, or our hair is not right, or our complexion is bad, or some of our body parts are the wrong size or shape. People don't usually compare themselves to Disney or other obvious fantasy characters. I've never heard anyone bemoaning the fact that they can't dance as well as Pinocchio or Cinderella. Is there any reason to feel badly that you can't dance like Paula Abdul and M.C. Hammer? Usually people don't worry about not having a figure or shape like Barbie, or Gaston in Beauty and the Beast. Are Dolly Parton and Arnold Schwarzenegger any less cartoon characters? That is not to say that these movie stars aren't perhaps real at home, but what we see on the screen is certainly not reality, and we shouldn't have to measure up to it.

The music world is just filled with fantasy. A singer from the 1950s named Ricky Nelson had an average voice, probably only good enough to sing in your church choir, as long as he didn't sing too loud. And yet, with the help of dubbing, sound mixing, and other studio magic, he sold thousands of records. More recently the "Milli Vanilli" duo received loads of awards for "Blame It on the Rain," until it was discovered they were just doing lip-synch. "New Kids on the Block," when accused of faking their music, first denied the charge, then claimed that because they were dancing so hard, they couldn't be expected to have the breath to sing at the same time. But therein is the fantasy — if they were to come out on stage and say, "We're really trying to dance and look cool, while a soundtrack of some other people's voices plays," then the fans could choose to accept that as reality or not.

In many ways rock and roll is just acting. Some rock groups don't actually play instruments — they are really just doing an "air band" up there on stage or on the video. Roger Daltrey of the "Who" says that he is playing a role in public that helps him sell records, but that he is nothing like that while "off the job at home." Many of the rude and rowdy rock stars are just acting outrageous to hype their image. In real life they may be fathers and mothers who take good care of their children, drive Volvos, and eat turkey on Thanksgiving. The sad phenomenon is that many young people are making life-style and moral decisions based on the fantasy being sold by rock musicians. It is tragic that a few young people have sought escape through suicide, perhaps partly because of the influence of some rock songs that promote that "solution." The reality may be that the singer/writer of the song is a forty-year-old guy living the good life in a mansion, driving a Corvette, who isn't the least bit inclined toward suicide, but who does the suicide tunes to make money.

Another example of a fantasy accepted as reality may be found in the scriptures. Book of Mormon people sometimes started believing that wealth made them better than those without it. By so doing, they accepted an idea that wasn't real — they were living in a fantasyland. "Some were lifted up unto pride and boastings because of their exceedingly great riches" (3 Nephi 6:10). Satan tempted them "to seek for power, and authority, and riches, and the vain things of the world" (3 Nephi 6:15). It's not that riches are evil in and of themselves. In Alma 1, the people are described as "exceedingly rich," and yet they remained loving, caring, and compassionate, and no one esteemed himself as being more important than his neighbor. In another place we read that "notwithstanding their riches, or their strength, or their prosperity, they were not lifted up in the pride of their eyes" (Alma 62:49). These people were not deceived or condemned, but those who were inclined to believe in the fantasy were warned: "And because some of you have obtained more abundantly than that of your brethren ye are lifted up in the pride of your hearts and wear stiff necks and high heads because of the costliness of your apparel, and persecute your brethren because ye suppose that ye are better than they"(Jacob 2:13). God's reality is that all of his children are of infinite worth. He has asked us to reject the fantasy world where people are "distinguished by ranks, according to their riches" (3 Nephi 6:12).

In today's media, fantasyland images show young, fit, happy people drinking beer. Is anyone in a beer commercial sad or quiet? The message of the commercials is that men who have just worked for eight hours on an oil rig, or who have ridden herd on some cattle, or who have played some high intensity basketball, don't need to shower. They just need to go to a bar and order some beer, and beautiful women will automatically mob them. The liquor fantasy is promoted as the path to having friends, fun, freedom, and fulfillment. The reality is that alcohol is associated with traffic accidents, family violence, trouble with the law, poor health, financial difficulties, unemployment, loneliness, and other negative realities that are never acknowledged in the fantasies created by the ad makers in behalf of the sellers of alcohol.

One of the great fantasies promoted by the world is that sex is a recreational activity. In this way of thinking, homosexuality, marital infidelity, immodest dress, and various forms of sexual expression outside of marriage are presented in positive, even glowing ways. Pornographic movies, books, and magazines present a fantasy world that is not just unreal, but also dangerous and destructive. If we believe that the Little Mermaid story is real, there is probably little harm. But if we accept the pornographer's lies, we will likely do significant damage to ourselves and perhaps to our loved ones.

Madonna and her agents have made millions of dollars selling her fantasy sex life in song, in films, and now in a best-selling book. Her public persona, carefully crafted to gain notoriety and money, seems about as real to me as the Wicked Queen in the Snow White tale, but a good deal more scary. In the story, the Wicked Queen's poison affects only one young woman—Snow White. The prevalent poison of immorality in our society is in fact destroying many beautiful, otherwise pure, young people. The reality of this wave of immorality is unwed mothers, sexually transmitted diseases, reduced self-esteem, promiscuous and unstable relationships, the pursuit of lust rather than love, and weakened spirituality. Our leaders have continually warned us against immoral behavior — explaining to us that its fruits are bitter.

God is real, and his commandments are based on eternal reality. If we will follow his counsel, we can enjoy loving, trusting, and intimate relationships within our marriages.

We ought not think that reality is dull, threatening, and without fun. A Calvin and Hobbes cartoon shows Calvin sleeping when his mother wakes him with, "You're going to miss the bus — now get out of bed!" In the next cartoon frame, Calvin's teacher is reprimanding him for not getting the right answer to a math problem. Later in the day, the school bully punches his lights out. Later, Calvin is not allowed to play after school until after he has finished his homework. At the dinner table he is ordered to eat his food without playing with it. Instead of toys after supper, he is sent to have a bath. Then, after the bath, his father turns off the TV and says, "No, you can't stay up a little longer — go to bed!" Calvin climbs into bed and pulls the covers up, his mother kisses him on the head, and says, "Have a good night's sleep — tomorrow's another big day!" The final cartoon frame shows Calvin, with a depressed look on his face. In the cartoon balloon above his head is just the sound, "SIGHHHHHhhh." We all have days like this, when reality hits hard, and some fantasy looks like a better alternative. But real joy and success are available only in the real world.

If reality is scary, challenging, stressful, or tiring, and you feel like it's just not worth it, you might need to get some assistance from a bishop, parent, advisor, or doctor. Consult with this trusted person about the things you are experiencing and feeling. Find out how to cope with and succeed in the real world rather than seeking to escape from it. Instead of turning to drugs or some other harmful retreat from reality, turn to God and his helpers here on earth, who know what is real. Sometimes getting away for a few hours in a fantasyland helps — a good book or movie might lift your spirits. But resist the temptation to take up permanent residence in a fantasy zone, especially one that is destructive and dangerous.

I knew a young man who had a good start on the gospel path, but who forgot, got careless, lost his hold on those realities, and abandoned the real world. He was an outstanding student, nearly always receiving awards for getting the highest grades in his school. He was a good-looking, healthy, athletic boy. He attended seminary and his Sunday meetings, planned on a mission, and was saving to help pay for it. He seemed to be well liked by others, attended parties and dances, and was getting to be comfortable talking and interacting with girls. But, when the benefits of living in the real world were not quick enough in coming, he was lured away to fantasyland. Early in his high school career, he withdrew from his athletics and exercise, prayer and church, his LDS friends, school, family activities, and finally, his home. He twice tried to withdraw from life.

Other young men his age have since achieved graduation from high school, completed missions, and are now involved in post-secondary education, marriages, families, and service in the community and in the Kingdom. He is only trying to stay employed, mostly in dead-end jobs that pay minimum wage. He is struggling to find meaning in life, mostly through booze and drugs. He is striving to find love, but mostly in casual, short-term relationships that end in stormy battles. He is searching for happiness, mostly in movies and videos that comfort him only while they flicker on the screen in front of him. He wants the security of a family, but mostly settles for fleeting good times spent with the children of women he briefly goes out with. He desires acceptance, respect, and popularity, and mostly gets noticed only for his outrageous behavior and clothes. He is on a quest for peace, and mostly has found pain, frustration, and emptiness. His life is filled with bad news. But the good news is that he can repent and return to the real world—the world that God has established where we might progress and find joy. We pray that he and all in his situation might do so.

Let me give you a final example to make the point. Let's say that you really wanted to attend the World Series or some other sporting event or rock concert. You haven't been able to get tickets, but go down to the stadium with the hope that you can buy one at the gate. They are all sold out, but as you turn to leave, someone offers to sell you a ticket. The ticket looks real, and is marked Zone G, Row 15, Seat 43. You pay what he asks, and go into the stadium. With the help of an usher, you find Zone G, walk up the aisle to Row 15, and move down the row in search of Seat 43. But the seats only go up to number 42! There is no Row 15, Seat 43! The usher examines your ticket more closely and determines that it is a counterfeit. You have been tricked — cheated, really — into buying a ticket that only *looks* real, but that doesn't represent a seat that really exists. You are not only escorted out of the stadium, and miss the show or game, but you are out the money you paid for the bogus ticket!

This parable describes what happens when people buy into a fantasy. Sooner or later, disappointment will come. That is what happens when we hold on to a hope in something like Seat 43. I pray that we are not fooled by fantasies, frauds, fallacies, and forgeries.

However old you are right now is a good age to confirm the reality of God's plan for you. Alma, Chapter 32, teaches us a grand experiment by which we can discover what is real. Experiments in the high school lab can render false results, if we handle the elements carelessly, or ignore the formula, or follow an incorrect procedure. But if we experiment on the words of God, as we are instructed in the scriptures, the correct results will come. "For the Spirit speaketh the truth and lieth not. Wherefore, it speaketh of things as they really are, and of things as they really will be" (Jacob 4:13). "O then, is not this real? I say unto you, Yea, because it is light; and whatsoever is light, is good" (Alma 32:35).

May we all discover that there is nothing more real than the light of the gospel, the love of our Father in Heaven, and the atonement of his Son.

Allen W. Litchfield is an institute of religion director in Edmonton, Canada. A former bank administrator, he has served as a seminary teacher and principal and as an institute instructor. Brother Litchfield enjoys reading and such sports as horseback riding and white water rafting and canoeing. Allen serves as a bishop, and he and his wife, Gladys, are the parents of six children.

13

REACH OUT! LIFT EACH OTHER! SOAR HIGH!

GARY R. NELSON

As my father exited the helicopter, a large lump formed in my throat. Teary-eyed and emotional, I wanted to hold on to this memory forever.

I ran out as far as the safety circle would allow to meet my somewhat breathless father and mother. I embraced my father.

"I'm so glad that I was able to do this for you, Dad. This meant so much to me."

"Thanks, Son," my father responded. "It was a neat flight." Pointing in the direction of the copter, he added, "He's a good pilot."

I had just helped my dad experience the fulfillment of one of his dreams—to fly in a helicopter. Owning a copter would have been better, but we settled for the next best thing. Ever since I could remember, I had heard my father talk about flying in a helicopter and about how much fun it would be to own one.

His dream became my dream; his passion for flying, my passion. That dream became a reality on September 19, 1992, a memory for my personal history book.

With a recently diagnosed muscle disease, my father's health was declining, and I was concerned that his physical strength would not permit a helicopter flight. As my heart turned toward his suffering, I remembered his dream. The timing seemed right. I decided to pursue his aspiration.

With the help of my good friend and former football buddy, Glen Bundy, I arranged for a helicopter ride for Dad at Bryce Canyon near Ruby's Inn. After several scheduling delays, my parents walked out to the helicopter with the pilot, Paul Cox, while my family and I anxiously stood by.

Paul opened the front passenger side door and assisted my mother to her seat. Then my large-framed father entered and straddled the back seat.

Can you imagine my feelings as I watched that precious cargo prepare to embark? My stomach was churning about as fast as the helicopter blades. Many thoughts raced through my mind. Would I ever see my parents alive again? Would they return safely? I was grateful for the calm, peaceful feeling the Spirit gave me.

The engine created a deafening roar, and the winding blades made a downdraft that kept my family and me at a safe distance. As my parents gave us their hesitant waves, the master pilot, who had over seventeen years experience without a single accident, moved the stickshift ever so slightly. The aircraft lifted off the ground, spun around in a 180-degree circle, then quickly ascended. When the pilot reached his predetermined altitude, he flew away over the trees and headed for a scenic overview of the Navajo sandstone formations.

I found myself caught up in the emotion of this exciting event. I had wanted to give something to my dad that he had wished for but never received. Now the magic of that event was nearly overwhelming. I felt an indescribable joy. I was grateful that my father had accepted the invitation, but as I served him, I was also lifted.

To reach out is to serve. To serve is to lift. To lift is to soar. Unselfish service results in inexpressible feelings of joy and love.

Reaching out is hard when we do not feel good about ourselves. Fear, a lack of self-esteem, no self-confidence, or something in our background or experience may rob us of our desire to serve others. The key is in the reaching. This is the first step. Instead of spending most of our time looking inside and doubting ourselves and our own inabilities, we need to look outside, look to others, reach out and serve. When we do this, both we and those we serve benefit.

We live in a day of quick, fast service. A day of convenience. We want it. We demand it. A day of fast food, drive-up windows, drive-up marriages, dial-a-prayers, lap-top computers, car phones, image-projected conference calls, fax machines, and sophisticated remote-controlled cable and satellite systems. A day of push-button luxury. In a day like this, taking the time to serve someone else may not seem convenient.

The opportunities to be of true service generally come at inconvenient times. It is not easy. Listening to someone's challenges takes time. Painting a widow's house, installing new tiles on a needy family's roof, visiting the sick, or performing any one of countless service projects—each requires effort and an investment of time. If we wait for the right day, the right hour, the right weather conditions, or just the right service project, we will miss many opportunities. Sometimes people need us *now,* without any strings attached. True service demands a willing heart, even if serving requires us to miss the Super Bowl, the World Series, or even a BYU football game.

Performing service can stretch our very souls, our very beings. The greater the effort, the greater the stretch, the greater the reward.

There is a principle in flying called "lift." Without it, airplanes could not fly. Aerodynamic lift is a force opposite of gravity. Gravity pulls the plane down, but lift allows the aircraft to rise. Lift is the upward force created by the flow of air passing over and under the wings. Airplane wings have a curved surface on the top and a flat surface on the bottom. The air going over the curved surface of the top of the wing takes longer to get past the wing than the air flowing under the flat side does. This creates greater pressure underneath the wing than on top of the wing, and the resulting lift is what makes flight possible. As the speed of the aircraft increases, the amount of lift increases.

To lift another person we need to overcome those gravitational forces that would pull us down—those things that prevent us from serving. Fear, selfishness, self-doubt, prejudice, pride, and sin are a few of the forces that tug on us, stifling our desire to serve and preventing us from lifting one another. King Benjamin taught that we need to overcome the "natural man" who is an enemy to God. (See Mosiah 3:19.) That natural man encourages us to take the easier road, the situation with the least amount of pressure. We need to counteract these forces by exerting ourselves in selfless service to others.

Lift, then, is a principle not only of aviation but of life itself. It affects the individual being lifted as well as the individual doing the lifting.

The lifting process is the serving process. In fact, according to King Benjamin, serving our fellow man is the way we serve God. (See Mosiah 2:17.)

By serving others, we not only bless their lives, we bless our own lives as well. The feeling of joy that surges through our soul and lifts our spirit is the soaring. And when we are soaring in and out of the clouds, wherever the breeze and spiritual currents take us, we can see the whole panorama below. This is something we would never have known or experienced had we not jumped aboard the service airplane. Everything now has meaning. From our new soaring position, we see the entire plan of Father before our eyes. Once one has experienced this higher vista of service, slogging along below through the heavy timber, thick scrub oak, and over the rocky terrain never satisfies.

"You cannot lift another soul until you are standing on higher ground than he is," said President Harold B. Lee. "You must be sure, if you would rescue the man, that you yourself are setting the example of what you would have him be. You cannot light a fire in another soul unless it is burning in your own." ("The Lengthening Shadow of Peter," *Ensign,* September 1975, p. 30.)

I recently witnessed an example of this reach/lift/soar concept: A high school I know about was planning to hold its annual senior ball. Excitement and hopes were high. The guys were making plans, and the ladies were hoping they would fit into those plans.

One senior I had taught as a sophomore wanted desperately to go on his first high-school date. He was backward socially and unsure of himself, but he finally garnered enough courage to ask a charming senior lady to be his date to the dance. She flatly turned him down. He ultimately asked four other young women, but each of them turned him down too. As often happens, his failure to get a date became the gossip of the school.

"Look out ladies, his next victim may be you," seemed to echo down the halls. And many girls purposely avoided him.

Although his spirits were dampened and his ego crushed, he got up enough courage to approach one last girl. She was a senior varsity cheerleader who was a student in one of my classes. She had not yet been asked to the dance. Ignoring the gossip, she accepted the invitation.

The young man was on cloud nine. He talked with me every day about his plans for the date he had made with this remarkable girl. He left notes for her. She responded with notes in return, furnishing him with information he asked for: her address, phone number, and the color of her formal. To say he was an excited man is an understatement.

The night of the dance finally came, and they had a great time together. She later told me, "Brother Nelson, that was not just *any* date. It turned out to be the very best date I have ever had." What made it the *best* date she had been on? He was struggling and in jeopardy of being crushed by disappointment. She recognized his need and had the courage to respond. In doing so, she lifted his spirits, and both soared high.

"Wherefore, be not weary in well-doing, for ye are laying the foundation of a great work. And out of small things proceedeth that which is great." (D&C 64:33.)

Those who seek to serve others would do well to ask themselves these questions: Why am I performing this act of service? Is it for selfish reasons? Is it so people will applaud my accomplishment? Is it so I can see my name and picture in the paper after a service project? Is it so this person will like me more? Is it out of duty, so that I can say that I have completed the task and check it off my daily "do list"? To whom does the glory belong? The Lord has said, "But when thou doest alms, let not thy left hand know what thy right hand doeth: that thine alms may be in secret: and thy Father which seeth in secret himself shall reward thee openly." (Matthew 6:3-4.)

In our attempts to be of service, we will do well to follow the Spirit. Then, instead of thinking about what we might get out of performing an act of kindness, we can concentrate on how the person we plan to serve will benefit and how we can bring more glory to the Master.

One of my favorite times of the year is Christmas. And one of my favorite family Christmas traditions is to read the Christmas story from the second chapter of Luke in the New Testament. We gather around a small nativity set, and as we read the narrative, each child takes a turn adding the appropriate olivewood figure to the scene. When Mary, Joseph, the shepherds, the baby Jesus, and all the other figures are in place, the nativity is complete. Well, almost. It remains for me to place my favorite piece of art amidst the hand-carved statuary—a ceramic Santa Claus, with his hat off, bowing before the Christ child.

One of the ways that I have enjoyed serving others over the years is to play Santa Claus. This way, I can serve anonymously. No one knows who is behind the beard, the wig, and the red apparel. I have been a welcomed guest in the richest of mansions and in the poorest of homes. I have played Santa for large shopping malls and for small home parties. I have donned the festive suit and visited hospitals, old folks' homes, ward parties, Hardee's drive-ins, and even roller-skating rinks. How many of you have seen a skating Santa? And yes, lest I forget, I even made one call on Christmas day!

I had my first Santa experience when I was an eighteen-year-old college freshman. Someone got the bright idea that because I was large in stature and a brawny college football lineman, I would also make a jolly Santa. (Bigger is not always better.)

I decided to go along with the pleadings of the college ward MIA group. It is hard to turn down cute girls, right, guys?

We went over to Cooper's Rest Home in St. George. We visited each room, handing the occupants a nice bag full of candy, nuts, and oranges. At first I felt embarrassed and uncomfortable. My "ho ... ho ... ho" lacked enthusiasm and sincerity. I kept asking myself, "Why am I here? Where did I come from? And where am I going after this activity is over?"

It didn't take long, however, to realize I was the star of the show. The elderly people were excited to see me. Once I realized that, I felt more comfortable.

The visit that really changed my life, however, was to a woman named Ruby. The walls of her room were covered with "foot-made" creations. I did not know how to react to her physical condition. Her head swayed back and forth. Her hands were bent and crooked, and she moved them back and forth in time with her head. Her feet were bare. And she was making a star *with her feet!* She maneuvered the paper between the blades of the scissors with her toes and somehow operated the scissors with the balls of her feet. She repeated this process until each cut-out was complete. Holding the finished Christmas star between the toes of her right foot, she extended her leg and "handed" me her gift.

I could not contain my feelings. I was spiritually touched. Like Joseph Smith, the emotion I experienced seemed "to enter with great force into every feeling of my heart." (JS–H 1:12.) I had reached out in a tentative, uncertain way, and I had lifted her somewhat by my presence, but she had lifted me in a way that made my whole soul soar. My feeble attempt to be of service resulted in a joyful experience for me. I was happy to be wearing the beard. It hid my tears. I left that room a changed person. I soared higher than an eagle — she had been the wind beneath my wings.

I got rather addicted to "Santa Claus-ing." I loved the feeling. And after my return from my mission to Brazil, I picked up *more* Santa experience.

One time I became involved in a local ward Santa program in which the Relief Society sisters dressed several Santas to travel around the ward on Christmas Eve. With the help of a priest-age driver, we made the rounds in our preassigned area. Each of us was given a large bag of navel oranges to distribute. I did not have many houses to visit, and I quickly finished my assigned visits, running out of houses before I ran out of oranges.

As we came around the corner of the last street, I spotted Miracle Manor, a neighborhood care center. "Why don't we stop here and give away the remaining oranges?" I thought. My driver needed to get home to a family Christmas Eve celebration, so I suggested he drop me off. After I finished I would walk the three blocks to my home in my Santa Claus suit.

The timing could not have been more perfect. Several elderly folks were gathered around a large blue spruce Christmas tree, opening gifts in the company of family and friends. I gave my new and improved "ho-ho" and made no small stir. Total commotion erupted. Little old ladies clustered around me, saying, "Santa, Santa, Santa," and the group spontaneously began to sing, "Here Comes Santa Claus." Several gave me hugs. I distributed nearly all my oranges.

Just as I was about to leave, I noticed a mentally handicapped young man sitting all alone in the corner of the room. He appeared to be about twenty years old and was without family or friends. I handed him an orange and wished him "Merry Christmas." I asked him the usual questions: "What's your name?" and "What would you like Santa to bring you for Christmas this year?"

"My name is Bill," came the reply. "But you're not Santa Claus. If you're really Santa Claus, then I want a *guitar* for Christmas. But I know that you're not Santa Claus."

"Oh yes, I am," I replied, a little uncertainly. "I'll see what we can do . . . You have a good Christmas," I mumbled under my breath.

I waved and walked out into the rainy night. Christmas Eve, 11:30 P.M., and the streets were deserted. As I walked home, all I could think about was "A guitar, a guitar for Bill. Where am I going to find a guitar on Christmas Eve?"

As I walked in the house, my wife immediately saw that I was concerned. "What's wrong, honey?" she asked. "Santa's not supposed to be sad on Christmas Eve."

"I know. But a guitar. Where am I going to find a guitar on Christmas Eve?"

She looked bewildered. By the look on her face I could tell she was thinking, "A guitar? What is he talking about?" I didn't have time to explain as a thought hit me. I realized where I might find a guitar.

My father owned a pawn shop. It was located in his sporting-goods store right below our apartment. I rushed down the steps, opened the door, and searched the room for guitars. I spied an old, red, classical, Stella, steel-stringed guitar with a black carrying case. I checked the pawn ticket and found the time agreed on for the owner to retrieve it was up. My father had loaned ten dollars on it. I put that amount in the cash drawer and ran back up the stairs. After a few minutes of waxing and polishing, the guitar looked like new.

In no time, I was back at the convalescent home, without Santa attire, holding the guitar case behind my back, trying to convince the female nurse that Santa Claus had sent me to deliver a gift to Bill at midnight. She eyed me suspiciously and suggested I come back during normal visiting hours. She looked like she was imagining I had a machine gun in the black case. I finally convinced her I was legitimate, and she motioned me down the hall to Bill's room.

Bill woke up as soon as the light came on. He sat upright in bed, rubbing his eyes. "Who are you?" he asked.

"I am a friend of Santa's, Bill."

"There's no such thing as Santa," he retorted in disgust.

"Oh yes, there is. What did you tell Santa that you wanted for Christmas, Bill?"

"A guitar."

"Well, here it is."

I drew the guitar case from behind my back, opened it, and handed Bill the shiny, red instrument.

"A guitar, a guitar," he exclaimed. "I have a guitar!" He hugged it tightly, and big tears filled his eyes and slid down his face, splattering on the guitar's shiny surface.

"Always remember," I said quietly, "there is a Santa Claus, Bill. And he loves you very much."

I left quickly with something wonderful bubbling up inside me. I had reached out. I had lifted. But the Lord had lifted me, and oh, how my spirit soared! As I knelt at my bedside with my beloved sweetheart later that night, I thanked Heavenly Father for the wonderful opportunity to be of service. "For inasmuch as ye do it unto the least of these, ye do it unto me." (D&C 42:38; see also Matthew 25:40.)

Now can you see why that kneeling Santa ornament in our nativity scene means so much to me?

The story does not end here. I checked up on Bill. The nurses said he took the guitar wherever he went. He ate with it, played with it, and slept with it. Wherever he went, he said, "Santa Claus is my very best friend."

Virginia Browning has written, "I lift thee, thee lift me, and we ascend together."

Someday, just like I happily embraced my father after his helicopter ride, we will be embraced by our Heavenly Father after our earthly journey. What a joyous reunion!

I bear you my humble testimony that true service rendered with a sincere heart and with real intent is one of the most powerful forces on this earth. It unlocks the heavens. By serving we become the Lord's hands. He permits us to do his work. Of this, I bear my witness.

I challenge you. Serve for the right reasons. Serve with all your heart, might, mind, and strength. Reach out, lift each other, and learn to soar high!

Gary R. Nelson, a seminary teacher in St. George, Utah, has been a seminary principal, travel coordinator, insurance agent, roller rink manager, motorcycle and mountain bike salesman, and a taxi driver. A former collegiate football and tennis player, Gary was a sportswriter for the Daily Spectrum, *and retains an interest in all sports. He enjoys writing, public speaking, singing, and going to BYU games. Brother Nelson and his wife, Christine, have seven children.*

14

BEAUTY AND THE BEAST: WHAT YOU'RE LOOKING FOR IS WHAT YOU'LL FIND

VICKEY PAHNKE

Did you ever wake up in a bad mood? You aren't even sure why, but you feel lousy? Isn't it weird that when you're having "one of those days," everybody else seems to get on your nerves? Then, when you are in a better frame of mind, everyone around you suddenly seems nicer? What is it that sneaks up on us, *inside,* and affects the way we see everyone and everything on the *out-side?* Could it be that the way we are looking at things makes the difference?

There have been times when I have seen things in a positive way, and created my own happy times. There have been a number of occasions when I could have used an attitude adjustment in order to make a bad situation better.

Have you ever had a day like this? I was thirteen. It was a hot, humid day, so I decided to go to the community swimming pool. I was in a bad mood, and hoped my spirits would be lifted. Nothing exciting was happening at the pool, so I grabbed my things and started across the field back home. Suddenly a sharp pain exploded in the back of my head. I saw stars and everything went black. I fell like a tree. Coming to, I looked up into the faces of several high school guys hovering over me. I had walked into the path of an informal football game. The quarterback was either a very good aim, or a very poor one, because his bullet pass caught me squarely in the back of my head. Talk about pain! They helped me to my feet and back into the pool area. To calm my nerves and regain my composure, I sat at the pool's edge, with my feet dangling in the water. Taking off my glasses, I laid them beside me, and leaned back to relax. A group of kids ran past me, and jumped into the pool. Not noticing my glasses, one of them took his last step on them, smashing them into many useless pieces. I couldn't believe it! Now I was in a terrible mood, my head was aching, and I was also blind! It couldn't get worse! (Never say this . . . it can.)

Some of my friends noticed my pitiful situation, and decided to help me out, by involving me in a game of leap frog. Have you ever played leap frog at the pool? If you ever do, make sure you are the "leaper" and not the "leapee." I was the "leapee," which meant I squatted at the edge of the pool while the "leaper" vaulted over my shoulders, and into the water. Only, my "leaper" landed on my back. I fell into the water, and scraped my shins along the cement as I went in. Now I understand why it is called leap "frog." I was frozen in a frog-like position, holding my sore shins, unable to move, and sinking to the bottom. When everyone realized I wasn't kidding, they pulled me out — a wet, bleeding, blind mass, with a terrible headache. Then they helped me home so that I could receive the required TLC from my mom, and calm my troubled nerves.

As I reflect on that day, I laugh when I think of how pitiful I was, and how awful I felt. The day seemed to be a total waste to me. Indeed, it was, and partly because I made it worse, by focusing entirely on the negative. I *was* blind, but not entirely because my glasses had gotten broken — I wasn't seeing things clearly because my attitude got in the way.

My friend Brad is color blind. Once, while on speaking assignment, several of us were riding together to the stake center where we were to speak. En route, another friend and I busily pointed out buildings and signs, asking Brad to try to identify the color. I was fascinated! Poor Brad couldn't tell blue from purple, green from blue. How sad to go through life unable to discern the true color of things! Then later that month, I went shopping.

(I do that on occasion just to keep in practice.) I found just the navy blue purse I had been looking for, and hurried over to show it to my shopping buddy. "It's nice," she said, "but it's not navy — it's black."

"Well, it certainly *is* navy," I responded.

I re-examined. She re-examined. We took it to the window to look at it in the sunlight. It looked navy to me, yet my friend insisted it was black. Then a thought struck me. Could it be that what I see, and think all people see, is only my perception? Do we all see things a little differently, colored by our attitude, our frame of mind, our point of reference? Are we all "color blind," from time to time, not seeing things as they really are? Maybe what I perceive is quite different from what you perceive — even when we are in the same location, at the same time!

What are we looking for?

Are we noticing the positive, the good, all around us, or are we sometimes blind to it? I believe that when we desire to look for the positive, our outlook can change. Maybe even the smallest adjustment in attitude can bring about a big change in the way we look at things, and how we feel about them.

Let's take a *look* at how we *look* at things. And at how we can *look* at them more carefully:

If we *look inside* with a sharper eye, we can *look outside* with a clearer vision. Feeling good about ourselves frees us from much of the ugliness of this world. A "can do" attitude even helps us be more successful in achieving our goals and desires.

A friend of mine I'll call Phil was totally reliable, very dependable, and likeable in every way. Phil had a problem with shyness, though. He never said much to anyone, and kept to himself. One day he came up to me, and while staring at his feet, said, "Vickey, guess what? I've decided to go on a mission."

"Phil, this is awesome!"

I hugged him, but then thought, "Phil, how is this going to work? You have to talk to people when you're on a mission."

Phil prepared, and was soon called to serve. He was excited as he entered the MTC, then the mission field. But immediately upon his arrival in the mission field, what do you suppose he was asked to do?

"I can't speak in front of a whole ward!" Phil wailed.

Because he was so full of fear and so convinced he would fail, he had never attempted to do anything like that. He needed to develop a whole new view of himself, and change his attitude.

The next Sunday, this "green" elder was expected to speak in sacrament meeting, and give a brief introduction of himself, and bear his testimony. He came to the pulpit, grabbed both sides firmly with his hands, leaned down into the microphone, and exhaled deeply. "Brothers and sisters," he began. Suddenly, *plunk,* his head hit the podium, and he slumped to the floor, at the feet of a very surprised bishop . . . out like a light!

The young Relief Society president came quickly up the aisle and knelt beside him. When he came to, he opened his eyes to see her finger pointed in his face, and he heard her say, "If you think you are going to get out of talking that easily, you better think again!"

Can you imagine? Though I at first thought she must be a heartless lady, I soon learned she was an inspired and loving leader, who understood that Phil needed a little help, if he was ever going to discover the potential inside him. She called Phil throughout the week, offering pointers and encouragement.

The next Sunday, Phil once more had the opportunity to stand in front of the congregation. He moved slowly to the pulpit, grabbed both sides firmly, and leaned down into the microphone. Could he accomplish the task? How could he live with this embarrassment? He breathed very deeply, and stared into the faces of the people who awaited his words. Every eye was upon him. Then, hesitantly and with a somewhat timid voice, he began to talk about himself, and to express his love for the principles of the gospel. Watching and listening to him was the young Relief Society president, who smiled encouragement and nodded approval, as this young elder did something that, just a week before, had seemed impossible to him.

At the conclusion of his brief remarks, he was elated! He had done it!

This was a turning point in Phil's life. He never thought he would be able to address large groups of people, but with effort, perseverance, and assistance, he accomplished a difficult task — to speak in sacrament meeting.

It is probable that Phil will not ever become a powerful public speaker, and he may never be entirely comfortable in front of large groups, but the experience made a difference in Phil's life. He was a better missionary, a better person, for the efforts he made. Most importantly, he learned he really was capable. He was able to *look inside,* and see more good there than he ever had before.

What a difference it would also make if we could all truly love each other — if we practiced the kind of love that builds up, and supports, and extends the benefit of the doubt. The kind of love that makes it possible to have no regrets about our relationships or how we treat a friend.

Cindy was my friend for years. She was beautiful, and funny, and sensitive. She had gorgeous, long, black hair that always looked perfect. Continually in a good mood, she seemed to have everything going for her. During our senior year in high school, Cindy began to complain of headaches. She missed school and her personality seemed to change. People began to wonder what was going on with Cindy — the consensus was she was being weird. Because we were her friends, we at first defended her, annoyed that our schoolmates could be so insensitive. Over a period of months, Cindy's difficulties continued. She missed more and more school, and was taken to doctor after doctor, none of whom could identify a cause for her headaches or personality change. She also saw counselors and therapists, but nothing seemed to help. After a time, even her closest friends lost patience with her, and also began to wonder, "What *is* going on with Cindy?" We withdrew our support from her, and when she quit coming to school entirely, we mostly went on with our lives, saddened that she had changed so, and was acting so differently.

One day we found out. She awoke with her eyes crossed. Her parents rushed her to the doctor. Tests were run. Cindy had a tumor that had grown so large it was pressing against her optic

nerve, causing her eyes to cross. She was hospitalized and prepared for surgery. We felt so awful for doubting our friend and
leaving her to cope alone during that terrible period of her life.
We wanted to put our arms around her and ask her forgiveness.
We were not permitted to see her before surgery, but her parents
told us she was most upset that her beautiful hair had to be shaved
off.

The surgery was completed and it looked good for recovery!
We were told her memory would be temporarily impaired, so she
wouldn't know us for a few days. We were excited to visit her,
anxious to apologize for our behavior, and hopeful she would soon
return to normal health.

The one warning she was given was to never try to induce
vomiting if she felt nauscous. The doctors feared the physical
strain might induce a hemorrhage.

We called her parents every day to inquire about her, so happy
for word of any improvement. In her second week of recovery,
Cindy was quite nauseous, did try to induce vomiting, and as
feared, she hemorrhaged. She lapsed into a coma and was placed
on a life-support system. Eventually, that life-support system was
removed. We never had the chance to put our arms around Cindy
and offer our apologies. We did not have a chance to be the friends
we should have been all along. I can't speak for my friends, but
I know how much I regretted my behavior. I learned that it is
important to be consistently loving, and to offer constant concern
and support to our friends.

Approaching life prayerfully also ensures that our vision is
clear, and our direction sure. Michael, my eight-year-old, is a
dynamo. He is energetic and funny, a whirlwind. Most people
would not be aware that he has had health problems. One night
several years ago, when just he and I were home, he awoke crying
because his legs hurt. I went to his room to find him tense, curled
up in pain. Rubbing Michael's legs, giving him pain reliever, plac-
ing him in a warm tub, all seemed not to help. Then I was prompted
to do what I *should* have done to begin with — say a prayer. Sitting
on the edge of the bed with a tense, crying Michael in my arms,
I offered a short, simple prayer. I wanted Heavenly Father to help

Michael, but I also wanted Michael to know that his Heavenly Father was there for him. In a split second, Michael relaxed in my arms. I opened my eyes to see a calm, comfortable little boy. Without opening his eyes, he said, "Mom, would you say a prayer and thank Heavenly Father?" For a mom, those were beautiful words to hear. Then he said, "Good night, Mom . . . Good night, Heavenly Father," and he drifted off in peaceful sleep. At that moment I knew that prayer was *real* to my four-year-old. I said a prayer of thanks, and oh, how I hope his faith in prayer will still be strong for Michael when he is fourteen, when he is fifty-four. If it is, his sight will be more sure, and his life more blessed. The scriptures give us the assurance that "the prayers of the faithful shall be heard" (2 Nephi 26:15).

By going to our Father in prayer, we can have our faith strengthened. Faith. A word often spoken, yet perhaps not well understood. What difference will it make in our lives if we not only *believe*, but *act* on that belief? If we look with faith, will the exercising of our spiritual muscles assist in clearing our sometimes clouded, temporal vision? Any difficulty we might experience can have an effect of either tearing us down or building us up. When life hits us hard, our faith permits us to look for the good that might come of our adversity. For people of faith, coping isn't just a process of surviving, but by successfully handling their problems, they emerge from their experiences stronger than before. (See Alma 14:26.)

I have a friend I'll call Janet. I met her when she was serving as a missionary in Virginia. She was a great example to many, with a true love for the Savior, and for everyone she met. She once told me that her dream was to complete her mission, find her "perfect" man, be married in the temple, and be a mom. Knowing her, I thought Janet would be the best mom ever.

We kept in touch after her mission. I soon learned that she and a wonderful young man planned to marry. I got news later that Janet had gotten married, and was now expecting a baby. I don't suppose there has ever been a more excited expectant mother! At the time of delivery, there was commotion and anticipation in the room. (There is great joy that accompanies the arrival of a new little one!) But the usual noise and excitement was noticeably absent after Janet's baby was born—voices of the doctor and the other attendants were subdued. The doctor handed Janet her newborn, and quietly said, "It looks like we have a problem here." It was then that Janet learned *her* child would not be like most others. Her baby was seriously physically and mentally handicapped.

Those in the delivery room hurt for Janet. As they thought about the ramifications of this less-than-perfect birth, their hearts ached for this new mother and father. But they were underestimating Janet's capacity for love and courage. As she tenderly held her newborn, Janet whispered reverently, "Oh, Heavenly Father sent me a perfect one. . . . He sent me a perfect one."

What a lesson was taught in that delivery room! Here was a woman who was grateful to be entrusted with the care of one of Father's purest spirits, one who is guaranteed entrance back to His presence. Janet is a wonderful example of how to look upon life's adversities with faith, understanding that our mortal view can be shortsighted and clouded. Eternal perspective allows us to see the beauty and blessing in everything—in everyone—around us.

Finally, I believe we would do well to look with our hearts. In the Old Testament we read: "For man looketh on the outward appearance, but the Lord looketh on the heart" (1 Samuel 16:7). He looks on our hearts, knowing our intentions, our limitations, our frustrations. He does not judge us by standards of this world. And he admonishes us to refrain from judging one another—or even ourselves, because we usually do not look with our spiritual eyes, and our vision is limited.

Not long ago, when I was at a speaking assignment in Las Vegas, there was a bit of free time. A group of us drove downtown, taking in the lights and the excitement of the "Strip." Have you seen it at night? The lights are dazzling, the buildings impressive. I thought of the many people who drive along that street and think, "Wow! This is beautiful! This is exciting! This is wonderful!"

Driving away from the Strip, we left the city behind, and drove up the hill toward the Las Vegas Temple. The contrast between real beauty and the tawdriness of what the world considers beautiful is probably no more apparent than in Las Vegas, since the temple was built there. We were privileged to go through a session, and as we later sat in the celestial room of that sacred edifice, I looked around and thought, "Wow! *This* is beautiful. *This* is exciting. *This* is wonderful." Driving back into town, my heart was saddened to think of all those who are deceived by the counterfeit "beauty" of the Strip. It is nothing more than a cheap imitation of real beauty. The garishness, the worldliness represented there, is not the way to true happiness. It is in the simple grandeur of the temple and its ceremonies that we find joy — not in the artificial neon world. If we are serious about being all we are capable of being, it is absolutely necessary to see with a clear vision. We cannot do it alone, but our Father stands ready to assist us. In the First Presidency's Christmas Devotional in 1986, President Ezra Taft Benson said, "Men and women who turn their lives over to God will find out that he can make a lot more out of their lives than they can. He will deepen their joys, expand their vision, quicken their minds, strengthen their muscles, lift their spirits, comfort their souls, raise up friends, and pour out peace. Whoever will lose this life to God will find he has eternal life."

The world is full of ugliness. There is much of pain, and confusion, and sorrow. If we are looking for peace or happiness in worldly pursuits, we will be disappointed, for the world does not know how to find it. Our Father's standards are constant. His ways are sure. He can assist us in obtaining a clearer vision of what will bring us happiness. As we learn to *look inside, look outward with love, look prayerfully, look with faith,* and *look with our hearts,* we will begin to see as the Savior sees. We will look for that which is good and praiseworthy (see Article of Faith 13). No, our lives may not be perfect, but the Savior is. And with his help, things will look a lot better, answers will be a lot clearer. We will begin to see things as they really are.

What *are* we looking for? It is my hope that we can help each other look for the best, the blessings, the beauty in life. If that is what we are looking for, that is probably what we will find!

Vickey Pahnke is a composer, musical and dramatic performer, recording artist, and lecturer. She is president of a production company and co-owner of a recording studio and serves on the board of directors for the Utah Special Olympics. Vickey speaks internationally on self-esteem and antidrug programs. Her interests include cooking, writing, laughing, and watching old movies. She and her husband, Bob, are the parents of four children.

15

FEELINGS: WHOA, WHOA, WHOA, FEELINGS

MATT RICHARDSON

Not long ago, I walked into my classroom to find two students pretending to be famous singers. They were swaying back and forth on their feet, and had their eyes closed. They were singing a song I hadn't heard in years. "Feel-ings, nothing more than feel-ings, trying to forget my feelings of love. Feel-ings, (this is where they began to really belt it out) wo, wo, wo, feel-ings . . . " In the middle of the "wos" they opened their eyes and discovered me standing in the back of the room, trying desperately not to laugh at them. I clapped wildly, and by the shade of their reddened faces, I knew they were definitely feeling *something!* They couldn't have picked more appropriate words for their situation: "Wo, wo, wo, feelings!"

I have occasionally thought about my "singing students," but it has been the words to the song they sang that have occupied my attention. "Feelings, nothing more than feelings . . . " This seems to tell us that feelings aren't that big of a deal. "Don't worry," they sing, "it's *only* your feelings . . . so you might as well forget about them!" What a tragic notion! If you take away your feelings, what do you have? *Nothing.* The truth of the matter is, your feelings are all you have that you can truly call your own.

Not only are feelings intensely personal and very individual, they are also extremely powerful. How many times in your life has excitement, anger, love, frustration, embarrassment, or shock molded the way you act? Take the feeling of excitement, for example. I was in Washington, D.C., for the Desert Storm victory celebration, and I had the opportunity to see the grand finale fireworks display. On the way to the park, a group of students and I laughed about the "standard fireworks dialogue." You know what I mean, don't you? What does every American say while watching fireworks? "Oooooh," and "Ahhhh!" What's really amazing is that you never hear two "Ooooohs" in a row. It's always, "Oooooh," followed by an "Ahhhh." I made a mental note not to "Oooooh" and "Ahhhh" during the fireworks – I was too cool for that!

The fireworks were spectacular! I had never seen fireworks like that before. I was so wrapped up in my excitement that I became only vaguely aware of someone tugging at my sleeve. I finally realized that one of my students was trying to get my attention, so I quickly turned and blurted out, "What?" "Chill out, Brother Richardson," was all he said. To my embarrassment, I realized that I was so excited that I had been screaming at the top of my lungs. I had not only been "Ooooohing" and "Ahhhh-ing," I had been screaming! "Look at that! I can't believe it!" And I had even utilized an occasional "Augggghh!" So much for being too cool! My excitement had driven me to act in a completely different way than I had planned (or even dreamed of).

You must not underestimate the power of your feelings. They are real. One of the most important things to understand about your feelings is that they can help you identify the truth. When it comes to discovering the things that really matter in your life, there is *nothing* that will assist you more than your feelings. I'm not saying that it's not important to read, study, think, and ask questions. These things lead to understanding the truth, but it is your feelings that will confirm what is right. This is how we gain a personal testimony. Bruce R. McConkie said, "The actual sure knowledge which constitutes 'the testimony of Jesus' must come by 'the spirit of prophecy' . . . Receipt of a testimony is accompanied by a feeling of calm, unwavering certainty." (*Mormon Doctrine* [Salt Lake City, Bookcraft: 1966], p. 785.) What a process! Study, ponder, act, and then, *feel.*

While traveling with his apostles, the Savior asked them, "Whom do men say that I the Son of man am?" They gave several answers, and after listening to their responses, Jesus asked, "But whom say ye that I am?" I have always loved what happened next. Simon Peter stood forth and boldly declared: "Thou art the Christ, the Son of the living God." What a fabulous, even miraculous, thing to say! How did Simon Peter know this? Wouldn't it be great to be able to honestly bear the same witness of Christ that Peter bore? Jesus responded to Peter's testimony by saying, "Blessed art thou, Simon Bar-jona: for flesh and blood hath not revealed it unto thee, but my Father which is in heaven." (Matthew 16:13–17.) Remember what Elder McConkie said? "Receipt of a testimony is accompanied by a feeling . . . "

I recall an experience I had while serving on my mission. While tracting, we found a man who grudgingly invited us in to talk with him. He was a large man, somewhat intimidating, and he sat on the sofa with his arms folded across his chest. He never broke a smile as he scowled at my companion and me. He had that "I dare you to teach me" look. During the course of our discussion, I looked this man square in the eyes and bore testimony that I knew there is a God in heaven who knows me and loves me.

He responded scoffingly, "So tell me, Mr. Mormon Missionary Man (that is what he had been calling me throughout our little conversation), when was the last time you saw this God of yours?"

With all my heart I wanted to tell him that it was only a day, a week, a month, or even a year ago. "I have never seen God," I sheepishly replied. Then remembering that I had a companion sitting next to me, I turned to him hoping that maybe, just maybe, he had happened to see God. Unfortunately he hadn't seen God either.

"Then you can't tell me that there is a God in heaven," our stubborn friend concluded confidently.

"I know there is a God in Heaven," I shot back.

"Okay, Mr. Mormon Missionary Man," he said, "when was the last time you heard God's voice call your name or speak some great message?"

I admit I was a little embarrassed as I told him that I had never heard God's voice. Strike two!

Our belligerent friend continued to taunt us. "When was the last time you touched God, or tasted God, or smelled God?"

I answered each of his mocking questions with, "I haven't."

I can still hear the sarcastic tone of that man's voice, and remember his taunting attitude, and I have never forgotten the feelings of resentment and inadequacy that he stirred up deep inside of me.

"See," he said again, as he leaned forward and pointed his finger at me. "You can't tell me that there is a God in heaven who knows your name and loves you. You just can't!" He smirked as he slouched back on the couch and refolded his arms.

At that moment, a feeling came over me that was perhaps a little like what Simon Peter felt. I straightened myself, looked him in the eyes, and told him: "I *know* there is a God in heaven who knows me and loves me. I just *know* it." By the world's methods of validation, there was no way for me to justify what I said. Yet, in my heart there was an undeniable feeling, confirming that what I said was true. I couldn't deny it. You see, my testimony is feeling-based.

This stubborn man of my missionary experience reminds me of Laman and Lemuel, who suffered from a similar spiritual ailment. They eventually became so hardened that they were "past feeling" and had to be addressed by the Lord with "the voice of thunder" (1 Nephi 17:45). Sure, they had the scriptures, had heard the prophet speak, and had even listened to an angel's voice, but something was missing. Elder Boyd K. Packer defined that missing ingredient when he said: "The scriptures generally use the word voice, which does not exactly fit. These delicate, refined communications are not seen with our eyes, nor heard with our ears. And even though it is described as a voice, it is a voice that one *feels,* more than one hears." ("The Candles of the Lord," *Ensign,* January 1983, p. 52; italics added.)

President Ezra Taft Benson has told us that "We hear the words of the Lord most often by a feeling. If we are humble and sensitive, the Lord will prompt us through our *feelings*" (*Come unto Christ* [Salt Lake City: Deseret Book, 1983], p. 20; italics added). When I was pressed to explain how I first received my testimony, I guess I didn't need to see, hear, touch, smell, or taste the truth. A *feeling* was good enough. My most memorable experiences are those closely linked with strong emotional feelings. Whether it was the thrill of playing sports, or the deep love for my sweetheart the day we were married in the temple, it was the feelings that accompanied those events that made them so precious, vivid, and real. By the same token, all the greatest experiences in my life have been accompanied by spiritual feelings.

Realizing how important and powerful our feelings are, we should be mindful that Satan knows the same thing. He fully comprehends that our ability to feel the Spirit is the key to our eternal happiness and ultimate salvation. Because of his knowledge, he will do everything in his power to destroy our ability to control our feelings, or what is worse, will strive to make us feel nothing at all. It is scary to look around and see how effectively Satan operates in this area. He is enormously successful in his attempts to influence what we feel and to erode our self-control. I have often been amazed at how successfully Satan influences those who ought to know better. As members of the royal and noble generation, you should know better. Latter-day prophets have marked you for greatness, and referred to you as warriors of the last days. Knowing your potential, Satan seems particularly determined to destroy your ability to feel the Spirit, and to deprive you of the blessings you have in store.

Perhaps this story will illustrate how Satan can destroy our self control. As a young man, I spent a week each summer at a reservoir, where my cousins and I lived in a mobile home. There were only a limited number of things to do there, and we often became bored. In our desperation for some excitement, we decided to try to ride some of the cows that were grazing on a nearby hillside. We snuck up on them (it's really not that hard to do, since cows aren't the most enthusiastic or intelligent creatures), and I attempted to ride one. It became immediately apparent that cows do not like people riding them. As a matter of fact, this cow freaked out! It began running, jumping, and twisting, all at the same time. I guess you could say it "had a cow," so to speak! Since I wasn't much of a rodeo rider, I soon found myself on the ground, nursing a bruised leg and a fractured ego.

My aunt and mother later picked us up and drove us to a store to buy some supplies. As they were shopping, my cousin and I began looking for a new adventure. A moderately steep cement spillway that emptied water into the reservoir caught our attention. I sat down in the water at the top of the incline, and whoosh! I was washed down the spillway and into the reservoir, about forty yards below. It was cold! But, after I had turned purple and caught my breath, I got used to the temperature of the water, and yelled for my cousin to slide down too. We pleaded with our moms to let us stay and play on the spillway, and they said we could, but that we would have to walk back to the trailer. (This seemed a small price to pay for something so fun.) We continued to slide down that spillway together until we knew it was time to leave. Our skin was so wrinkled, we must have resembled giant California raisins. We laughed as we walked along the roadside back to the trailer. To our surprise, every car that drove by us from the rear, honked at us. We smiled and waved wildly! We were impressed by the friendliness of the locals. As we walked, we began to thaw out and regain our natural color. I remember starting to feel uncomfortable on my backside, so I reached back to see what the problem was. To my horror, I found that my jeans were worn away and there was nothing but a big hole in my cut-offs. To make matters worse, I had worn through my underwear as well. I was horrified! I looked over at my cousin and he was in the same awful predicament. The passing cars weren't just being friendly, they were honking at two idiots with holes in their pants, walking down the road (and to think we waved back!).

I learned a very valuable lesson from that embarrassing experience. The water was so cold it made me numb to feeling anything. And, lacking my normal ability to feel, I had no sense that each trip down the spillway wore away part of the seat of my jeans—thread by thread. My cut-offs didn't wear through in one slide, it only happened little by little, and without my knowledge. I didn't even see it coming. How embarrassing!

I have found that this "revealing" experience has much in common with the tactics Satan uses on us. He slowly numbs us and then gets us involved in activities that gradually wear away at our appropriate feelings. We don't even see it coming. "We can handle it," we say with great confidence, or "Only once won't hurt," we jeer. We think we are so smart, so in control, but in reality we are playing the most deadly of games; little by little we become numbed, and thread by thread, our ability to feel can be worn away.

This is why viewing some types of movies is so destructive. Scenes in such movies cause you to feel things that may be inappropriate. Such feelings, if unchecked, can ultimately destroy our sensitivity to the Spirit. The same goes for music, alcohol, drugs, or television. If you are involved in substance abuse you soon get to the point where you cannot feel the spirit of God. To tell you the truth, you can't feel much of anything—other than the temporary effects of the drug. Meanwhile, Satan laughs while he pats himself on the back, because he knows that if he robs us of the ability to feel the Spirit, then the Lord can't reveal his truths to us. We are thereby deprived of the chance to experience genuine happiness. He knows that if he can only get you "past feeling"—like Laman and Lemuel—he wins. Remember that Satan doesn't need to be in any hurry. He is content to destroy us, thread by thread.

The time has come to say, "whoa" to those destructive feelings. The time has come to take charge, straighten up, and get in control of our feelings. It is frightening to think about the number of people who react solely to what they are feeling, those who let their emotions control their lives, or those who are so numb that they can't feel, or don't care. So how do you start to feel again or get your life back into control? Maybe we should start by planting the seeds of appropriate feelings. This is what Alma talked about in Alma, chapter 32. Put something worth feeling into your heart and then let it grow. Help it grow! Get the weeds out of your life by getting in control of your life. Cut out those things that cause you to get angry, feel immoral, or think impure thoughts. Find something that you already know is true—or hope to be true—and then share it with someone else. It really doesn't matter what that something might be. You might hope (or know) that there is a God in heaven. Maybe you have a testimony of honesty, or of keeping the law of chastity—share it! It is by bearing our testimonies that we cause them to grow. I have found that I feel the Spirit most strongly when I speak from my heart, and tell people about spiritual truths. I feel closer to those I love when I tell them how I feel about them. Let those feelings expand, share those feelings, permit them to grow!

When you start to feel the workings of the Spirit in your life, you will find the greatest joy you've ever experienced. Will you please let those feelings continue in your heart? Sometimes we have a tendency to cut the spiritual feelings short, to put a stop to them because they are new or different than anything else we have felt, and maybe even a little frightening. Some people begin to feel uneasy with spiritual feelings and don't know quite how to act. Please, let those feelings swell in your heart. Don't laugh, or get up and leave. Please don't say a word or drive those feelings away—just sit back and feel. I promise you, it is a feeling that will enrich your life forever. It will grow, and fill your heart with hope, if you let it and encourage it. This is why I can look people in their eyes and tell them, "I know God lives, Jesus is the Christ, and that the truth gives me hope!"

May I extend Alma's invitation? Plant a seed of feeling in your heart, and then let it grow, share it, and help it grow. Guard your feelings with all your might. They're yours. Your feelings are your key to happiness and a strong testimony. I know that our Heavenly Father and Christ live, and that they love me, just as I know they love you too. I *feel it* and hope you will too!

Matt Richardson is a seminary instructor in Pleasant Grove, Utah. A candidate for a Doctorate of Education, he is also a part-time instructor at Brigham Young University. Brother Richardson has taught Danish at the MTC and has helped develop national drug-free programs. He enjoys playing all kinds of sports, cartooning, watching old movies, and studying advertising and communications. Matt and his wife, Lisa, have three children.

16

LOVEST THOU ME? FEED MY LAMBS

KATHRYN S. SMITH

It was a fast Sunday. Church wouldn't start until midmorning, and so I was nestled at my computer, enjoying a few quiet moments with my journal before it was time to clang the bells and get everyone up to get ready. My youngest daughter, also an early riser, marched firmly into the kitchen. She surveyed the obvious lack of breakfast, and without a word she pushed up her sleeves, grabbed open the refrigerator, and emptied it of eggs, milk, and bacon. She opened the cupboard, grabbed the frying pan, and slapped it down on the stove.

"Becca," I began in the gentlest of mother voices. She was ten years old. "It is fast Sunday." Strains of the Tabernacle Choir drifted sweetly across the room.

"I know!" she barked, not slowing her progress toward the feast she envisioned. I smiled inside, enjoying the moment. I had several options here: I could put everything away and send her stomping off to her room to ponder the joy of the fast, or I could attempt to awaken her conscience and allow her to use her agency. Preferring the latter, I tried mother-lecture number 204:

"Becca, don't you want to show Heavenly Father that you love him by obeying the fast?" I batted my eyelashes and smiled sickeningly.

Her response was quick and two-edged. "He knows I love him! I'm hungry!"

She never missed a beat. The bacon went on sizzling, and the eggs scrambled deliciously. I looked up at the ceiling, having one of those *Fiddler on the Roof,* Tevye moments, and prayed. "She's your daughter too. *You* zap her conscience!" Apparently something touched her, because she has never done that again, but her words have echoed down through the years.

How often do we say to ourselves, "Heavenly Father knows I love him, but I'm hungry?" Or, "I want to be part of . . . to fit in." Or, "It won't hurt this once—I can close my eyes during the bad stuff—Heavenly Father understands." This is faulty thinking, if only because others are watching—some of whom will be influenced by our choices.

Do you know that after the Savior's resurrection some of his apostles went back to their fishing boats? They'd been called on a mission, but they didn't know what to do now that Jesus was gone. John the Beloved left us this account:

Peter, John himself, Thomas, and four others had climbed into their boat one evening and fished all night long. There were no supermarkets in Palestine—if they wanted breakfast, they had to go find something to eat. The morning sun broke over the Sea of Tiberias and we can all imagine the glistening color on the water, and the mixture of shades of red in the sunrise. On the beach, there was a man watching them. None of them recognized him, but he called out, asking them, "Children, have ye any meat?"

"No," they hollered back.

He called again, "Cast the net on the right side of the ship, and ye shall find."

When the net was again in the water, the fish swarmed into it. So many, the net should have broken from the strain.

At this point, John recognized the resurrected Savior, and said to Peter, perhaps in a reverent whisper, "It is the Lord."

Peter—so wonderfully passionate and strong—immediately dove off the side of the ship and swam through the waves to shore. The other apostles rowed in, towing the net full of fish behind them.

The Savior had prepared a fire of coals, on which he was roasting fish, and warming bread, and he said to them, "Come and dine."

After they had eaten, the Savior fastened his eyes on Peter the way he might fasten them on you or on me, and asked, "Simon, son of Jonas, lovest thou me more than *these*?" There, lying on the shore, was a great net full of fat, flopping fish. What did the fish represent to Peter? They were his livelihood, weren't they? They were his income—they were his comfort zone. They represented what he was accomplished at doing, what he knew he could do well.

" . . . Lovest thou me more than these?" Jesus asked. Do you love me more than the things that make you content? Or the things you do well? Or the things you enjoy doing? Do you love me, even if that love requires you to get out of your comfort zone?

There stood Peter, perhaps still wet from his swim to shore. His face might have fallen, saddened that Jesus would have to inquire about the nature of his love. And he responded, "Lord, thou knowest all things; thou knowest that I love thee."

I can feel a pause in that still morning air, and imagine Jesus' face taking on a look of tenderness as he gave Peter his charge — not once, but three times—"Feed my lambs. . . . Feed my sheep. . . . Feed my sheep" (see John 21).

What did the Savior mean when he gave that commandment?

Like my daughter, Becca, everyone is hungry. What do we feed each other? Do we toss each other Twinkies, eager to be the comic, the one with the flashy smile? The one with the quick answer—the quick fix? Or do we nourish?

One evening our family was enjoying a summer barbeque. The food steamed on the counter—the corn on the cob, the burgers off the grill, the salads, the chips, the condiments for the buns. Each of the children had gone through the line, filling their plates with whatever they wanted to eat, and my daughter, Tarisse, then about eleven, had been first in line. She sat down and took a bite out of her hamburger. She told me later that as she chewed, she realized that something was missing. She couldn't figure it out, but the sandwich tasted different than she had anticipated. She opened it up and saw the catsup, the mustard, the lettuce—she must have forgotten to add one of the seasonings she liked, but she was unable to determine what. As I sat down beside her, she looked at *my* hamburger to see what she might be missing.

When something is missing in our lives, we naturally look around to see what others have. If someone seems content and happy and fulfilled, while we are discontented, unhappy, and unfulfilled, we will likely watch them to try to figure out what it is they have that we don't.

A young Latter-day Saint was a successful athlete in a small-town high school. He was a good kid and a good competitor, but no matter how well he performed, his coach constantly chided him because he was "straight"—because he didn't participate in the typical after-game activities of the other guys. His language was different, his attitude was different, and the coach noticed the separation, and commented on it constantly. It couldn't have been any worse if the coach had publicly exclaimed, "What do you do after our games—go home and play Barbies with your sister?"

All through the young man's high school athletic career, the sarcastic jibes continued, so that the boy dreaded any encounter with his coach. The first week of his senior year, he went to pay his deposit and pick up his football equipment and uniform. He was given some change, but quickly stuffed it into his pocket and left, so the coach wouldn't have time to make one of his usual remarks.

It wasn't until he got home that night that he noticed he had been given too much change. A dollar too much.

"Oh great," he thought to himself. He could see it now—waving the dollar in the air and singing, "Here coach, I'm so honest. Here is the extra dollar you gave me!" No way. He wasn't about to set himself up for more ridicule. The coach had just lost a dollar.

The next morning came, and because of the kind of kid he was, the young athlete realized that he couldn't keep the money. He made his way as inconspicuously as he could to the coach's desk, and laid down the dollar bill.

"You gave me too much change back," he mumbled, and then tore for the door. He was an athlete, and he intended to use his speed to get out of there before the coach would have time to say too much.

As he ran away, he heard the coach bark out, "Pay up!" Startled, the boy stopped, and turned to see his coach standing with his open hand extended to his assistant coach.

What the young Latter-day Saint hadn't realized, but suddenly became aware of, was that he had been set up. He had been given back a dollar too much on purpose. And his gloating coach had bet his assistant *one hundred dollars* that the "Mormon kid" would bring the dollar back.

People *are* watching you. Can they bet on you?

Back to the family barbeque. I finished fixing my dinner plate, and the last item I put on my hamburger bun before I covered it with the top bun was the meat. "That's it!" Tarisse squealed, "I forgot the meat!" She explained her predicament, we laughed, and got the meat for her burger. It tasted much better then. Do you realize that when people are spiritually hungry, they are usually missing something substantial, like the meat? We make a mistake when we toss each other "junk food," on the mistaken notion that everyone wants "dessert." The truth is that the best thing we have to offer to others is our core beliefs.

Do you expect those who are observing you to come up to you tearfully and exclaim, "I am so grateful for the example you have set for me. Your righteousness has been a beacon of light that has beckoned me onward . . . "?

NOT!

Many times people who observe a good example feel a little resentful—watching someone with high ideals may make them feel embarrassed because they are incapable at that point of living equally well. That doesn't mean your example is not being observed or that people are not betting on you to be strong. Albert Schweitzer once said, "Example is not the main thing in influencing others—it is the only thing."

I know a young man named Brian who, after he had graduated from college, began to take flying lessons from an LDS pilot friend of mine. Brian was determined to become a Navy bomber pilot and he eventually achieved his goal. He now flies A-7 bombers and was named the Student of the Year during his training at naval flight school. He is obviously a very good pilot today, but those first lessons were still his first, and he was as much a beginner at that point as anyone.

One afternoon, in the middle of a flight lesson, Brian asked my friend, "Can you teach me about religion? All I have ever known about Jesus is what I have seen portrayed on television at Christmas time." The missionary lessons were arranged, and they were held in my home. Brian was as golden an investigator as I have ever seen. He read the Book of Mormon, he listened to the elders, he questioned them earnestly, and he prayed for a testimony. It did not come. As I prayed for him, I wondered why the confirmation was withheld.

I did not know then that when Brian was in high school he had had some LDS friends. They partied together, but he was aware that on Sundays his Mormon friends would go to church and bless the sacrament. None of them ever thought to invite him to church. They did not realize that Brian was spiritually hungry. Instead of inviting him to the main meal, they had tossed him Twinkies. And they not only excluded him from the feast, they provided a horrible example for him.

He took note of that example. As he later listened to the missionary discussions in my home, he held back his heart because he wondered if anyone *really* lived the Word of Wisdom.

One night, after a particularly touching lesson, Brian committed to baptism. He had still not received his witness, and I asked him why he had made his decision without it. "Perhaps if I join the Church," he explained, "Heavenly Father will believe that I am sincere, and will answer my prayer." I was profoundly touched by his humility. He was baptized, and when he came to church he would sit with our family. He continued to read the Book of Mormon, and we had great talks about what he was learning. I knew his testimony was growing, even if he did not recognize it yet.

Then it happened. One of the elders who had taught Brian the discussions had completed his mission, and the night before he was to fly home, Brian visited him to say goodbye. There is a bonding that develops between missionaries and their converts, and Brian loved these guys. They were having a fun chat until, at one point during the visit, Brian went to get a drink of water. In the refrigerator where the elders kept a pitcher of cold water, he discovered a can of beer!

What Brian didn't know was that in an effort to help an investigator commit to living the Word of Wisdom, the elders had gotten him to give them a six-pack of beer to dispose of. Thinking it would be a funny trick to play on the missionary who would be coming to take his place, the elders had put a can in the refrigerator, and had forgotten it was there.

But there it sat, and even as long as a month later, Brian sat at my table with tears streaming down his cheeks. "Kathy, the elders who taught me the gospel drink beer!" It made no difference what I said. My explanations didn't convince him. He did not believe me. When he closed the fridge, he closed his heart, and he walked away.

What is in your spiritual refrigerator? When people who are hungry come to you, what do you have there to feed them? That can of beer could just as easily have been a dirty video. It could have been a swear word. It could have been an off-color joke. It could have been gossip, or a show of anger. Do we follow the Savior's request to feed his lambs? Or do those who come to us go away hungry?

.Dr Stephen Mecham served as president of the Finland Helsinki Mission during the time the Berlin Wall fell, and at the time the doors were opened for missionaries to first enter Russia to preach the gospel there. In a fireside held for LDS Religious Educators in Southern California, he said that the people who had been liberated by the opening of the Iron Curtain are so hungry for the gospel that 80,000 missionaries could be put to immediate use there. One couple was so intensely interested in the gospel that they offered to finance transportation for the elders to come to Siberia, to teach them the discussions. President Mecham consented to the trip, and when the elders were met at the station, this Siberian couple said, "We hope you don't mind, but we have invited a few of our friends to listen to the lessons with us." When they arrived at the building that had been arranged, 800 people were waiting to hear the first discussion. They are hungry.

President Mecham explained that before the missionaries entered any town to teach, he would visit the government officials to obtain legal permission to organize a unit of the Church there. He told about trying to obtain a license for the elders to work in a town in Estonia. The city officials were skeptical about admitting representatives of a foreign religion. Their state religion seemed adequate to them, however, they agreed to think about the request overnight and to make a decision the following morning.

One official had an appointment later that same day with an American newspaperman from Chicago, Illinois. After they had concluded their business, the Russian asked the newspaperman, "You're an American. What do you know about this Mormon religion?" The gentleman from Chicago responded by saying that he was not a member of the Church himself, but that his best friend was—and that he had never met a finer man or a finer family.

The next morning President Mecham met with this group of officials, and the one man stood and said: "I met an American yesterday, and he told me that this religion creates fine families. I think we should let them in!" And so they did. President Mecham told us that somewhere in the city of Chicago is a wonderful LDS family whose members, though they are not aware of it, are responsible for the Church being allowed to preach the gospel in a town in Estonia, Russia. What was in their spiritual refrigerators? Do we ever know when people will open the door? What will they find on our shelves?

In Springville, Utah, a group of ten boys was born into the same ward during the same year. None of the families moved away, and so these young men grew up together, attending the same Primary classes, priesthood quorums, Scout troop, and schools. They found different interests as time passed, but they remained friends. In the spring of their senior year in high school, just after the snow had melted off the roads, one of these young friends hopped on his motorcycle and accidentally crashed. With a head wound, he was rushed to the hospital, and his hair was

shaved off to examine the damage. It turned out he was not
critically injured, and so he was sent home—bald and stitched up.
This young man was seventeen years old. He was a senior in
high school. Prom was coming up. How could he return to school
looking like a porcupine head, with a scar and stitches nestled in
the fuzz just beginnning to grow out of his scalp? Can you feel
what he must have felt?

Was he hungry? Was there something missing?

One of the other boys, Todd Jackson, phoned the other eight
young men in the group and told them to meet him at the barber
shop. You can finish the story—they all got shaved bald and then
showed up together at their friend's house. "Come on. Let's go
to school!" I suspect there were ten porcupine heads in atten-
dance at the prom that year.

Speaking in April Conference in 1992, Elder Marvin J. Ashton
said, "The best indicator of our spiritual progress is the way we
treat each other." I often hear mocking laughter in the halls at
my school as students put each other down. I watch some of them
avoiding kids who are different, and only surrounding themselves
with people they are comfortable with. What good does it do us
to have a testimony, if we don't reach out and lift one another?

When my family moved to Utah four years ago, none of my
children had attended school anywhere but in Albuquerque, New
Mexico, where we had lived for twelve years. My second daughter
was a sophomore in high school when we moved, and she stepped
into the halls of Provo High School, not knowing even one other
student. At lunch that first day she heard someone call out her
name. "Tarisse!" She knew no one would be calling to her, but
she was curious to see who else had her name, because she had
never met anyone else with it.

There, over a sea of heads between them, she saw our next-
door neighbor, Chris Clark, who was a senior. In fact, he was the
student-body vice president.

"Tarisse, come here!" He was gesturing to her! She made
her way through the crowd, and he grinned at her, putting his
arm around her shoulder.

"Come here, I want you to meet some of my friends." He

guided her over to a couple of benches filled with smiling faces, and he introduced her to them, one by one. She didn't know whether to be horrified or pleased. Every day Chris would come and find her and include her in his crowd. He insisted she try out for the school play, and she made the cast. He watched out for her like you would a lost kitten, until he was sure she had found a niche. And then he drifted off, friendly, but no longer attentive. Do you think he did that because *he* needed to be noticed? Everyone in the school knew his name. Not only was he a student government officer, he had been one of the leads in every important theatrical production each of his four years at Provo High. In the yearbook Chris was voted "most friendly" by all the girls in the school, and it was obvious he was not stepping outside his normal behavior in his approach to Tarisse. I believe he reached out to my daughter because he understood the profound reality that all of us are hungry to fit in—to be "part of"—and he was willing to help a new kid on the block.

The Savior taught us that when he comes again in all his glory, all the nations will be gathered, and he will separate them as a shepherd divides his sheep from the goats. And what will be the criteria he will use to separate those who will inherit the kingdom of his Father from those who will not? I don't think he will look at our clothes, or our muscles, or our skills. I don't think he will ask to see our bank accounts or the cars in our garages. I think he *will* evaluate the quality of our hearts, for he has said, "I was an hungred, and ye gave me meat: I was thirsty, and ye gave me drink: I was a stranger, and ye took me in: . . . Inasmuch as ye have done it unto one of the least of these my brethren, ye have done it unto me" (Matthew 25:35–40).

"Hast thou not known? hast thou not heard, that the everlasting God, the Lord, the Creator of the ends of the earth fainteth not, neither is weary? . . . He giveth power to the faint; and to them that have no might he increaseth strength. . . . But they that wait upon the Lord shall renew their strength: they shall mount up with wings as eagles; they shall run, and not be weary; and they shall walk, and not faint" (Isaiah 40:28–31).

Kathryn S. Smith is the mother of four children and a middle-school teacher of English and French in Provo, Utah. She has been an early-morning seminary instructor and has had such diverse experiences as studying at the University of Grenoble in France and teaching Chinese cooking at the University of New Mexico. A world traveler who, in 1966, toured around the world in ninety days, Kathryn's many interests include the theater, writing, and horseback riding.

17

"IF I'M WEARING THE WHOLE ARMOR OF GOD, WHY DO I KEEP GETTING BEAT UP?"

A. DAVID THOMAS

One heartache of being a teacher, father, and friend is watching people you know and love having to cope with cruel and abusive experiences. Some of these mistreated people are among the sweetest and kindest individuals I have ever met, and one wonders why life should impose such unfairness on them.

One pleasure of being a teacher, father, and friend is being able to observe how many of these noble and great souls have refused to allow the brutality and unkindness they have experienced to break their hearts or tarnish their dreams. Those who soar above the cruelties of others learn, as their elder brother Jesus showed, that the glory comes from nobly carrying our individualized cross. But one still wonders—"Why are some people so unkind?" And maybe an even more appropriate question is, "Have I ever been so cruel?"

As a teacher, father, and friend, I have had the opportunity to observe the best and the worst of human behavior. I have been both a receiver and (unfortunately) a distributor of abuse. My heart aches as I observe my children and others I love and care about either abusing others or being abused. What can be done about the ugly problem of abuse?

A disturbing characteristic of the "natural man" is the tendency to take advantage of weakness. Some people seem almost compelled to identify those whom they classify as "different" and to bully them in some way. Sometimes this discrimination manifests itself in cruel treatment, but no matter what form abuse takes, abuse is ugly, unbecoming, and wrong. Sometimes an abuser is seeking an outlet for his own shame and rage. He takes some kind of twisted pleasure in making others grovel by imposing his unkindness on a helpless victim. If we are to believe reports in the media, abuse is becoming more common, and it involves emotional, physical, and sexual mistreatment.

All of us know how it feels to be designated as a human victim. Janis Ian put it this way:

> To those of us who knew the pain
> Of valentines that never came,
> And those whose names were never called
> When choosing sides for basketball.

All of us have been left out or have been made to feel foolish because someone held us up to ridicule and made us feel unacceptable. Abusers wear such unattractive hats as

1. A teacher or an adult who minimizes or discredits your dreams.

2. Any person who demeans or humiliates you.

3. Any person who betrays a trust or takes unfair advantage of you.

4. Any person who, to aggrandize himself, downgrades others.

5. Any person who doesn't respect your personal space and your right to be you, just as you are.

6. Anyone who seeks to belittle your faith and beliefs.

7. Anyone who inflicts harm on you, whether it be physically, spiritually, emotionally, or sexually.

8. Anyone who chooses to attack your views and perceptions or who tries to force you to see and accept their world view — be it the reality of Santa Claus and the Easter Bunny or UFOs.

It's abusive if someone treats you in a way that keeps you from being you or tries to inhibit your free agency. Furthermore, to the extent that the abuse prevents us from being what God intends, abusers are enemies of God, and we know who they serve. Truly, Satan is the father of abuse, and abusers are his children.

Has it occurred to you that those who gossip are abusers? That those who punch and push around a weaker comrade are abusers? How about those who point their fingers to identify someone they perceive as inferior to them? Perhaps we have all been guilty to some extent of these kinds of behavior. But the moments we probably remember most vividly are those moments when someone has abused us. We abusers apparently have selective memories

One sad truth is that abuse can breed abuse. All abusers, we've been taught, were once or are presently being abused in some way. The cruelty they inflict, it would appear, is simply an outlet for anger they feel because of the cruelty they have experienced. Unkindness is taught because it is tolerated and practiced. The devil sings and we listen when we let cruelty live.

It is easy to find and explain the need for victims in the animal world. Victimization serves a purpose in nature. It thins the herd, or feeds the hungry, or mercifully removes those ill-equipped to survive by animal rules. Kill or be killed is an article of faith for animals. Cruelty serves a purpose in the jungle, but it has no purpose among the children of God.

When I was in high school I saw animal cruelty firsthand. I worked part time on a mink farm. Now, mink are raised for their fur. Many women would love to have a mink coat. Without a doubt, the fur of a mink is a wonderfully soft thing, and petting a mink would be a pleasant experience if they'd let you hold them. But they won't. Mink are savage animals. They love to bite, and they have razor sharp teeth. They seem to hate everything, even their own brothers and sisters. Baby mink are called kits, and when the mink kittens are born they look as precious as any other kind of baby, but they are born mean. From their birth they fight and bite. Sometimes their fighting and biting draws blood. Fresh blood to a mink is like a red matador's cape to a bull—it drives the mink crazy. One of my jobs was to find the blood-covered kits, those injured in fights with their brothers and sisters, and to cover their wounds with a medicated powder to mask the taste of the blood. If the wound is not medicated, covered with a smelly powder, the victim's brothers and sisters will often kill the wounded animal.

In human behavior the medication we use is just common kindness, the application of the "Golden Rule" — dispensing the sort of kindness we yearn to receive. But despite our best efforts, life will continue to be mean right up until Jesus returns. The Prince of Peace will eliminate all unrighteousness and put an end to abuse. Until that day we must strive to overcome our own capacity for cruelty and work to put an end to abuse in general.

How do we do that? Consider this story.

In early spring of 1951, a young movie starlet by the name of Debbie Reynolds was called to the office of her boss, Louis B. Mayer. Louis B. Mayer ran M.G.M. studios, and a call to his office was a big deal. Debbie entered fearfully, but Mr. Mayer was smiling. He told her he was pleased with her work. The studio, he explained, was now going to feature her in her first starring role and her co-stars were to be Gene Kelly and Donald O'Connor, both of whom were already famous entertainers. Debbie was a fan of both men, and she was thrilled. The movie would be called *Singing in the Rain*. She was also told that Gene Kelly, the movie's star and director, was on his way to meet her. Right on cue, Mayer's secretary "buzzed" and announced that Kelly had arrived. He was sent right in. Kelly had no idea why he was there, but as he entered he said hello and was totally charming to Debbie.

Then Mayer dropped the bomb. "Gene, meet your new co-star."

Kelly could only stare dumbfoundedly. He was a consummate performer, a wonderful dancer, and a perfectionist who suffered over every detail of his movies. He matched himself with dancers the way a horsebreeder might match bloodlines, and he knew nothing of this young woman's work.

"Do you dance?" he asked hopefully.

"No, . . . well, a little," Debbie answered.

"Do you sing?"

"Not really," she timidly replied.

He then asked her to stand up and said, "Do a time step." Debbie complied by doing the only step she knew, a waltz clog, while Kelly grew even more agitated. He corrected her mistake; and his tone clued the young performer and would-be-dancer that she was "coming up way short." Finally, he asked irritably, "Can you do a maxi ford?" (Kelly's favorite step). You can imagine how he must have reacted when she answered naively, "I don't have a car."

Now, Gene Kelly didn't want to be unkind or abusive, but dancing is a hard, even a cruel, craft. The price of being really good is high, and he had earned his reputation by long years of hard work. He looked dejectedly at Louis B. Mayer and asked, "L.B., what are you doing to me?"

Unfortunately for young Debbie Reynolds, Louis B. Meyer had a plan — a plan that would force Debbie through the abuse of becoming a dancer quickly.

The studio had only a few weeks to get nineteen-year-old Debbie Reynolds "up to speed." O'Connor and Kelly's skills were the result of a lifetime of dancing and learning, but L.B. Mayer's plan was to cram that much skill and learning into Debbie in just three months! Three teachers were assigned to work with her in shifts — Ernie Flatt, who would one day choreograph "The Carol Burnett Show"; Carol Haney, Kelly's assistant and the future star of the Broadway play *The Pajama Game*; and Jeane Coyne, who would soon be Mrs. Gene Kelly.

For eight hours a day, the three shifts of teachers hammered dancing into Debbie. It was not just a matter of learning to dance; Debbie had to become skilled enough to perform with two of the entertainment world's truly exceptional dancers. Day after day the training went on. Blisters formed over blisters on her feet and then finally broke and bled into her shoes. Her body ached, and her heart yearned for some comforting words. She needed some assurance that she was improving and would one day master her task. But everyone was too busy. There was so much to do and no one had the time to encourage the "want-to-be dancer."

As the deadline approached, her emotional mercury began to boil, and finally she exploded with rage, removed her shoe, and threw it across the room with such force that it shattered a wall of practice mirrors. She was exhausted, disheartened, and humiliated. Needing to be alone, she found an empty sound stage and there under a grand piano she let it all out. She sobbed, and sobbed, and sobbed.

Debbie was interrupted by a voice. A man asked simply, "Why are you crying?"

She choked back her tears and looked out from under the piano. All she could see was a pair of immaculate trouser legs and some expensive shoes. She said, "I'm crying because I'll never learn any of it. I can't do it anymore, and I feel like I'm going to die. It's so hard. I can't . . . I can't . . . ."

"You won't die," the voice counseled. "That's what it costs to learn to dance." Debbie crawled out from under the piano and looked up into the concerned face of Fred Astaire. He gently helped her up and said, "Come and watch me."

Now, nobody was allowed to watch Fred Astaire practice, not even Louis B. Mayer. But Astaire knew the price of dancing, and he wanted to validate Debbie's effort. She watched as he rehearsed for a new movie called *The Royal Wedding*. And guess what. He cried. He got angry. He developed blisters on the blisters on his feet, then his blisters broke and stained the inside of his dancing shoes with blood. As Debbie watched she discovered that life is painful and hard, even abusive, for everyone, even dancers like Fred Astaire.

Even the gifted have to pay the price for success. There is no shortcut to mastering geometry or ballet. Being human is not always easy, and all of us must pay the price for living here. Some of the abuse we encounter in life is nothing more than the dues we must pay to claim our right to be ourselves. We can cry and moan, or we can endure. It's up to us.

But what about abuse and pain that seem to have no purpose? What about abusers that ravage children? How do you explain Hitler and other dictators who inflict cruelty on a huge scale on their helpless victims? There are people who drown kittens and tie cans to puppies' tails. Some cowardly persons draw courage from numbers and secrecy and wear hoods while railing against minorities whom they despise because of race or religion. And what about mobs of three and four who stalk defenseless kids at school, corner or provoke them, and then inflict injuries? There can be no doubt that there is much cruelty and violence in the world. Men, women, and even children harm each other in nearly unspeakable ways.

Even so, we must not participate in this great evil or permit ourselves to become violent or cruel in response. There are things we can do:

1. *Practice empathy.* Empathy is the ability to feel compassion. It involves putting ourselves in the place of others, trying to see and feel things from their point of view. If we are able to imagine the pain our actions might inflict, then we will be less likely to act in a cruel fashion. Remembering our own fears, we might seek to comfort rather than to frighten others.

2. *Form a network of strength.* We can band together in groups to resist abuse in all its forms. We can speak against it and stand up in opposition.

3. *Blow the whistle!* So many of life's bullies prosper because no one challenges their crimes. Stand up! Be heard! Blow your whistle and call a foul! Get help if you can't handle it. That's why God invented bishops and society invented police.

4. *Forgive.* Although cruelty and its results are wrong, only *you* pay for hating. Once the evil has passed and you are safe, vacuum your soul of the natural hostilities that live there. Forgive and grow.

5. *"Lift your lamp."* Use your bad experiences to create good ones. You have moved out of the grasp of abuse, but don't just be an enemy of evil, be a source of answers — a solution. Become a guide. All great teachers learn from their experience.

By contemporary standards, Walt Disney was abused as a child. The abuse was not sexual, and many of his contemporaries were similarly abused at a time in history when "spare the rod and spoil the child" was the prevailing philosophy of parents. Walt's father ruled with an iron hand. Elias Disney, like his famous son, was a man with a head full of dreams, but, unlike Walt, he lacked the imagination and internal "whatever" to make them happen. He failed at raising oranges in Florida. He failed at being a contractor in Chicago. He would fail at farming in Marceline, Missouri. And his investments in newspaper distribution and a jam factory would fail too. He took out on his family the frustration generated by his failures. He inflicted whippings on his sons and required abnormally hard work of them. To escape his tyranny, Walt and his brothers all eventually ran away from a home where there was an abundance of corporal punishment but not enough love.

At a point when only Walt and his older brother, Roy, remained at the Merceline farm, and when typhoid from their well water had felled Elias, the management of the farm was left to the two remaining brothers. Roy was sixteen, and Walt was only eight. The two boys were overwhelmed. There were no frivolous books for distraction. Life seemed to consist only of unkept promises, hard work, and a belt. The two older boys had escaped, Herbert at nineteen and Raymond at seventeen. They had fled their father's world of failure and despair. Elias never laughed. His face always disapproved. He was an icy presence with no sense of fun. Fun, in fact, was prohibited. It had to be sneaked into. No candy. No Santa Claus. Nothing fun to read or games to play.

Walt obviously somehow found fun. He always saw Merceline as his "laughing place," but never with the approval of his father, and the belt was always there. Walt found two ways to escape — by observing nature and by spending fun time with his Uncle Ed. Out of doors, Walt found life and light, fun and animals. Ed brought joy, candy, and laughter whenever he visited.

Ultimately, all his brothers ran to escape the gloom and abuse inflicted on them by their father. Their midnight departures caused great pain to Walt's mom, Flora, and to the rest of the family. Finally, it was Roy's turn. Late one night, Walt discovered his older brother packing for his early morning departure. As he prepared for his escape, he gave Walt some counsel: "Don't let him hit ya, kid. Stand up for yourself!" The counsel was all Roy, only seventeen, could offer his little brother. Walt loved and trusted Roy, and he ultimately followed his brother's advice.

One day Elias forced Walt into the basement for an unwarranted beating. Recognizing the injustice of the situation, Walt wrestled with his father for the belt, ripped it from his hands, and threw it to the ground. Defeated by his youngest son, Elias collapsed in tears and shame, and he never tried to beat Walt again.

Elias's tyranny took other forms. Walt worked for his father on the farm and in the numerous other attempts his dad made to become a successful businessman. Though the hours were excessive and the work very hard, Walt was never paid. His father kept all the money. Walt yearned for control of his own life and resources — for freedom.

Finally, he found an excuse to leave. The First World War was underway, so Walt lied about his age and, though only fifteen, joined an ambulance corp. He never lived with his father again until he was a man, and then only on his own terms. He was safe, and he set out to fill the world with the fun his dad had always deprived him of.

So, dancers, actresses, visionaries, and cartoonists all may experience abuse. Scriptural heroes have also gone one-on-one with abuse. Joseph was sold into Egypt by his heartless brothers, and Nephi had to contend with the cruelty of Laman and Lemuel. Esther was challenged by ruthless Haman and fought against his vicious ambition in order to save her people. Joseph Smith confronted abuse almost daily. And Jesus, our brother and Savior, validated his concern for us through the abuse he suffered. Abuse in some form or another seems to be our common lot. Some suffer more than others, and only our Heavenly Father can explain why. But we can soar above it by practicing empathy, having courage, developing our gifts, and increasing our capacity to forgive. Walt Disney did.

In 1957 Disneyland was opened to the public. It was the product of the heart and genius of Walt Disney. In its creation he gave expression to all the things his father thought were useless. It should be noted, however, that Walt came to understand the source of Elias's disposition and outlook. It was his father's failures. And to forever dispel that failure, Walt re-created the main street of Merceline, Missouri — his "laughing place" — and made it the entry way of his joyful theme park. On Main Street in Disneyland, on the left side, on the top floor of one of the buildings, there is an office. It looks like the office of a successful businessman, and the sign on it reads: "Elias Disney, Contractor."

Look for it the next time you visit Walt Disney's gift to us all. It is the evidence that Walt understood and forgave his dad and a reminder that Disneyland is the town that forgiveness of abuse built.

A. David Thomas is a seminary principal and teacher in Park City, Utah and an instructor of business at the University of Phoenix in Salt Lake City. Holding a Ph.D. in education, Brother Thomas has taught in youth and family programs at Brigham Young University. David is the author of There Are No Dragons Out There, *and beside writing, his interests include reading, running, and traveling. He and his wife, Paula, have six children.*

18

"BE OF GOOD CHEER"—YOU KNOW WHAT AMMON KNEW!

PAULA THOMAS

I love to read. I especially love to read about the lives of people—people who have survived heartache; people who have survived difficult times. People who, like the Phoenix in Greek mythology, seem to rise from the ashes of abuse or despair and somehow make something significant and even courageous out of something hurtful or dark. As I read and study about the lives of people like this, there is something deep inside of me that causes me to desire, or almost believe, that even I could do something brave or of worth, something maybe even significant.

I grew up in the fifties. That was a time when there was no doubt about who the heroes were. It was very simple: the hero, or the good guy, always won and he was always fighting for "truth, justice, and the American way." Superman was a great example. He was faster than a speeding bullet, stronger than a locomotive, and could leap tall buildings with a single bound. Each week he came into my home on TV, overpowered another bad guy, and made the lives of all good people involved a little better because he had been there. Boy! did I want to do that. Not fly like Superman, but have the power to make someone that was sad—happy; or someone that was poor—rich; or bring friends to someone lonely. Even though my desire to be the hero was great, real life made being heroic just a little more scary than it seemed to be for Superman, or Zorro, or Hop-a-Long Cassidy. I always seemed to fall short of heroic deeds, because of fear. Fear that I would look stupid; fear that I would be physically hurt; fear that my friends or peers would not agree with my stand, and I would be left alone — the fear of all fears!

It seemed to me as I turned the pages of the books, or watched the hero win another battle on the movie screen, that he knew something that the other characters in the story had not yet discovered. His insight or knowledge was something that gave him the courage to rise above the others. Fear did not appear to dictate to him when or when not to move.

Ammon was one of the four sons of King Mosiah. He and his brothers were friends of Alma the Younger. For several years these young men battled against God's church on earth, setting aside the teachings of their fathers. After their conversion and a painful repentance process, all five young men went on a mission to preach the gospel to the Lamanites. They all went their different ways, all being guided by the Spirit. Ammon ended up in the land of King Lamoni where he was captured and brought before the king as a Nephite spy. The penalty for this crime was usually death, but not in this case.

King Lamoni sensed there was something different about Ammon and asked him if he (Ammon) desired to dwell in their land among their people. Ammon told the king that he wanted to stay, but he wanted to stay as a servant to the king. I doubt that King Lamoni had people lining up outside his door applying for position as servant.

His wish was granted. Ammon was sent along with the other servants to tend the flocks of the king. All of the servants of King Lamoni, except for Ammon, knew how dangerous this job was. Rebellious Lamanites would frequently attack the king's servants, then steal and scatter the sheep. Failure to protect the flocks was intolerable to the king, and he had his unsuccessful servants put to death. You can imagine how these men dreaded having to face Lamoni if they had to report the loss of some of his sheep.

One day Ammon and his fellow servants were doing their jobs when, like so many previous times, a group of hostile Lamanites attacked and proceeded to steal and scatter the king's flock and to run into the forest with their newly acquired goods.

Ammon watched the servants of the king as they stood helplessly by and began to weep because of their fear of being slain.

"Now when Ammon saw this his heart was swollen within him with joy; for said he, I will show forth my power unto these my fellow-servants, or the power which is in me, in restoring these flocks unto the king, that I may win the hearts of these my fellow-servants, that I may lead them to believe in my words" (Alma 17:29).

I love this story! I love Ammon and what I have learned from reading about his experiences. Ammon wasn't joyful because he saw these men so fearful, and he didn't feel joy because he felt superior – he felt joy because of the potential he saw in the situation. He saw that the Lord could turn this difficult and even frightening moment into an opportunity to share the gospel with his fellow-servants, and maybe even with the king. Ammon had been given a "teaching moment." If his courage and physical strength were impressive, and he were asked about the source of his prowess, he could truthfully attribute his success to the Lord's assistance, and then teach the gospel to his admirers. He wasn't being arrogant – he was seizing a missionary opportunity.

Ammon knew four things of great worth: (1) He knew of God's love and concern for all people on the earth. (2) He knew that Jesus Christ was the son of God and he understood the Savior's mission. (3) Ammon knew that in God's strength (with his guidance and prompting) he could do all things (see Alma 26:12). And, finally, (4) Ammon knew that he was an instrument in God's hands and that his life had purpose and meaning (see Alma 26:3).

At this point in our story Ammon counseled the king's servants to "Be of good cheer." He could say that because he knew that God would back his play and that the lives of his fellow-servants would not only be spared, but that they were about to receive a great and wonderful gift – the gift of light and knowledge. They would be taught what Ammon knew.

The other servants watched Ammon as he chased the enemies of the king. These men did not fear Ammon, for he was only one and they were many. Ammon cast stones at them with his sling and in this manner killed six of the intruders. Observing his courage and power, the rest of the rebellious Lamanites became frightened. They ran toward him with their clubs, but each time they raised their arms to strike Ammon they would lose an arm by Ammon's sword.

The servants of the king were astonished at what they had witnessed. They ran to tell this miraculous story to Lamoni and the result was that Ammon had been given an opportunity to teach the gospel to King Lamoni, his household, and his people. Because Ammon listened to and followed the promptings of the Spirit, many believed his words and embraced the eternal truths.

I admire Ammon and view him as a great hero, like so many others whose stories we read in the Book of Mormon and the Bible. His physical performance is not what I base my opinion on, but rather what was inside him, that gave him the courage to perform. He lived what he believed.

How many times have you been in situations that you felt were wrong, but didn't dare let anyone know you felt that way? How many times has foul language been used in your presence — especially the Lord's name in vain — when you voiced no objection? How often have you listened to a friend or an acquaintance tear down another friend or acquaintance, or share with you a little piece of juicy gossip, without your preventing it? I know in my life I probably couldn't count the times I have allowed these kinds of things to take place. I either lacked the courage or hadn't yet sufficiently defined my beliefs. In either case, I failed to act as I should have.

On the other hand, I can't begin to tell you of the joy and power I have felt on the few occasions when I have performed as Ammon did — when I have acted on my convictions and have testified about the things I believe.

One of these times was when I was eighteen years old. I had graduated from high school and was just beginning to attend college. I was taking a philosophy class and religion became a topic for discussion. The class was large — about 250 to 300 students —

and we met for our lectures in a large auditorium. Most of what was taught that quarter went right over my head. I did, however, understand the section on religion. The unit focused on how the great philosophers felt about God and the basic principles that religious leaders had been teaching for centuries. We discussed several ancient prophets, including Noah and Moses, and questions were raised about whether or not there was a flood, or if the Red Sea was really parted.

One morning Jesus was the topic of discussion and his identity was called into doubt. Some in the class concluded that, while he was a great teacher of moral and ethical values, he was certainly not the Son of God. I listened as the debate became more and more negative. I had already obtained a witness for myself that Jesus was the Son of God and the Savior of the world. The fact was, I felt like I had come to know him personally—he was my best friend. My faith in and love for Jesus were the things I depended upon to lift me in my down times, to give me courage when I was afraid, and to fill my soul with hope when life seemed hopeless. As I listened to members of the class, tears welled up in my eyes and a giant lump wedged itself in my throat. My heart began to pound so hard and fast that I just knew it was only a matter of time before it leaped from my chest.

Much to my surprise I found myself standing in the center of the auditorium, having been compelled by the Spirit to testify of what I knew. The words were not mine; they were carefully chosen and filled with meaning and impact. When my testimony came to a close, I ended it in the name of Jesus Christ—the very One who had been the center of the debate; and I returned to my seat. I felt my face grow hot and flushed. I found, in the silence, that I began to feel embarrassed. Then I began to wonder what other people were thinking.

The teacher dismissed the class and I stood to leave. As I worked my way out of the row of seats, I came face to face with one of the most profound learning experiences of my life. I was approached by so many people expressing their appreciation for saying what they too had felt, but hadn't been able to bring themselves to say. The phrase I heard most from students in the auditorium that day was: "I'm so grateful that someone had the courage to speak out, I only wish it had been me."

We shouldn't have to express regrets like, "I wish it had been me." We need to have the courage to seize the teaching moments that present themselves. We don't always have to verbalize our testimonies. How we *act* can have a profound effect on others — for good or bad. We must choose. Ammon's joy came from being given the teaching moment. He knew that his response to a difficult situation would attract attention. He had his testimony and he had the courage to act — to use the circumstance to do what the Lord needed done.

There are times when the Spirit acts on us in a quiet and personal way, not to bless the lives of others so much as to strengthen us and increase our faith. My nineteen-year-old son had such an experience with the Spirit that helped him more fully understand the power of prayer. One cold March day, he was playing basketball with his younger brother and a friend behind a local school. A van drove up behind the school, and a woman got out and approached them. She explained that she was looking for her pet bird. This was a special bird. It had been part of their family for years, but the bird had flown out a door that had accidentally been left open. She handed the boys a flier with the description of the bird and her phone number printed in large letters. My son is a lover of all kinds of animals, and he instantly felt a great deal of compassion toward this lady, who was obviously hurting. As he stood on the playground watching her drive away, he felt prompted to silently pray, "Please, help me find this bird for this family." He wasn't only asking for help to find the bird, he was also saying, "Heavenly Father, if you are really there, help me find the bird." He was asking for his own belief to be strengthened. He returned to the basketball court to finish the game.

The weather for the next two days was not good for a bird that had lived in a house all its life. The family had been told by experts that the bird would not know how to forage for food or how to protect itself from the weather. Chances for recovering the bird looked fairly bleak.

A couple of days after his encounter with the lady, my son went to work at the video store where he is employed. It was a snowy afternoon and he was working outside the store, retrieving tapes from the drop box to return them to the shelves. As he was emptying the drop box, he saw what appeared to be a dead pigeon lying up against the glass front of the building. As he reached down to see if it was still breathing, the bird climbed onto his hand, crawled up his arm, and began to speak to him! He recognized immediately that he had found the lost bird. Filled with joy and excitement, he rushed into the store to call the family that had lost the bird, and that by now must have nearly given up hope.

"Hello. Mrs. Marshall, this is Jim Thomas. I've just found your bird!"

He heard cries of excitement and gratitude over the phone as Mrs. Marshall conveyed the news to her family.

Well, what do you make of the experience? A bird that was poorly prepared to survive was lost. My son said a prayer that he might find the bird. He found it, and returned it to the concerned family. Some would say it was only good luck that the bird survived and was in a place to be found and returned. But my son sees it differently. He perceived a need. He prayed for assistance. The prayer was answered. And the effect of the experience is that my son's faith in prayer is stronger than before. Believing this, he is a little more prepared for his next experience with the Spirit, and he is more likely to ask again. This is the way the Lord dispenses his blessings—"line upon line, precept upon precept; here a little, and there a little" (D&C 128:21). The key is always, "Do you believe?" If so, then the Lord seems willing to grant another portion.

If you can stand in a testimony meeting and say, "I know God lives and loves me. I know Jesus died that I might repent and live again with my Father in Heaven, and I know that my life has purpose and meaning," then you can say, "I know what Ammon knew," and if you truly believe, you will be one of the heroes of the future.

Paula Thomas has worked for Brigham Young University youth and family programs for nine years. A mother and homemaker, she is working to complete a degree in family science at BYU. Sister Thomas has served as a ward Young Women president and been involved with the Governor's Conference on Drug-Free Youth and Families. Her interests include reading, writing, and caring for her family and home. She and her husband, David, both authored a chapter for this book. They are the parents of six children.

DATES WITHOUT PITS

BRAD WILCOX

Kim was my date for the Junior Prom. I was enjoying our dance together. I didn't notice her corsage fall. I only noticed that something was under my shoe. I thought it was someone's gum. I slid my foot against the floor like it was part of a new dance step. When the song ended, I escorted Kim to the side of our school gym. As she looked down, she exclaimed, "My corsage! Where's my corsage?"

Pushing my way back onto the dance floor, I cleared the spot where Kim and I had been dancing. There was the corsage all right, but it was obviously dead. I reclaimed the wilted, battered flowers, and walked them back to Kim. "Here," I said, pinning them back on her.

"What are you doing?" She seemed startled.

"Look," I explained, "my dad paid good money for this thing."

That evening was a long time ago. But, I still laugh when I think of our dance picture. There I am, smiling broadly. There is my beautiful date, in her lovely prom gown. And there, drooping from her dress, is this pitiful weed.

Everyone has similar, funny-now-but-awkward-at-the-time, experiences to share when recalling past social situations. Some dates come with pits. However, there are some things we can do to take the pits out of our dates. Here are four suggestions that can easily be remembered by thinking about the letters of the word D–A–T–E.

D STANDS FOR DIFFERENT

Outsiders don't have to be around Latter-day Saints long to realize that we are different. The scriptures call us "peculiar" (1 Peter 2:9). Some people come up with even more colorful adjectives to describe us, and as long as they are not cutting, we shouldn't mind being described as being different.

For instance, we're the only people I know who hold meetings called "firesides" in buildings that don't even have fireplaces. Have you ever tried to explain to your friends why you called a lady in the store "sister," while you call your real sister a "MIA maid," and why neither of them is offended? My friend Steven Kapp Perry points out, "We are the only people around who, once a month, don't eat anything for twenty-four hours and then we have a meeting about it so we can breathe on each other. And they call it a 'fast' meeting—It's the slowest meeting in the Church!" Imagine an investigator's confusion when the leader of the twelve-year-old girls stands and tearfully says, "I just love my Beehives!" If someone backs out of a driveway and runs over the cat, most people would consider it a total tragedy. But not Mormons. We smile through our tears and say, "There has to be a lesson to be learned in this!"

We *are* different. We're supposed to be. Addressing members of the Church, Peter said, "Ye are a chosen generation, a royal priesthood, an holy nation" (1 Peter 2:9). The expectation is that we will stand out and be a light to others (see Matthew 5:14–16), and not simply blend in with everyone else. That is why it is no surprise that LDS dating standards are different from those of the world. We do not date until we are sixteen. We date in groups and avoid pairing off exclusively with one partner. We date only those who share our same high standards (see *For the Strength of Youth*, [Salt Lake City: The Church of Jesus Christ of Latter-day Saints, 1990], p. 7).

I hope it won't be offensive to make an analogy of dating to what we know about cows. If you have ever been on a farm you have probably seen cows with their heads through the fence, trying to reach the grass on the other side. Those fences are there for the safety and protection of the cows, and while most of them graze contentedly in their own pasture, a few can always be found pushing against the barrier, testing the boundaries, and straining to reach the feed on the other side of the fence.

LDS dating standards might be compared to pasture fences. Dating guidelines have been established to provide for our safety and protection. The ground inside is spacious enough; there is plenty of room for enjoyment and growth inside the boundaries; we needn't push up against the barriers. By attempting to reach something we imagine is better or more appealing on the other side of the fence, we put ourselves in danger, and risk missing what has been provided us in the field we have been given.

I remember an LDS girl in our high school whose parents were in agreement that she should not be allowed to date until she turned sixteen. It seemed to her like all her Mormon friends were successful in getting their parents to ignore the rule. They would argue, "But the bishop's daughter isn't quite sixteen, and they let her go to the dance." Or, "But I'll be sixteen soon—what difference does a few months make?" And some *parents* even rationalized, "Perhaps the prophet is thinking about *maturity,* and not necessarily just age; and our daughter is *very mature.*"

While many Mormon kids (and their parents) pushed against the fence and even broke through, this particular girl's parents said, "No way." She wasn't just up against a fence. She was running into a brick wall. My friends and I decided to help her survive the last thirty days before she turned sixteen, and would be able to legitimately date, by having a little fun with her. We wanted to help her be content to stay in the middle of the field.

A month before her birthday, we started a countdown. On a tiny piece of paper we wrote, "30," and taped it to her locker. She looked at it when she got to school, picked it off quickly, and went on her way. The next day, she found a larger paper on her locker. The number was, 29. Each day the numbers got smaller, and the papers got bigger. By the time we got to 5, she couldn't even see her locker. The hall looked like Sesame Street! Finally, on her sixteenth birthday, we presented her with a list of dates for the next week—a different guy every night. We didn't even skip Sunday when we made sure she had a date to go to a fireside. By the end of the week she was so worn out she wondered if she ever wanted to date again.

When I was growing up, we were also counseled to date in groups. Once, my friends and I got a group of about twenty-six people to go to a movie together. The lady selling tickets just about had a coronary. We had to wait in line for the movie to begin, but we didn't wait in a line. No, we're Mormons. We waited in a circle. The guys stood on the outside of the circle, and the girls on the inside. Then, every two minutes I'd yell, "Change!" and the guys would all rotate one girl to the right, and start a new conversation.

My friends and I went on many such group dates, inviting lots of different people to join us. Of course, there were couples who always refused to join us, because they were glued to each other — more out of insecurity and low self-esteem than love. They were pushing against the fence and running into all kinds of barbed wire. We, on the other hand, were in the middle of the field having the time of our lives.

Another Latter-day Saint expectation is to date only those who hold high standards. This isn't always easy. One young woman from an area where the congregations of the Church are not very large told me, "There is only one guy in my whole city who is a member of the Church, and he's a deacon!" Such difficult circumstances do not change the counsel of the First Presidency. We will be blessed if we stay in the center of the field — even if we sometimes feel as though we're there all alone, with just the deacons.

"But, what about missionary work?" one young woman asked me. "My aunt's, cousin's, brother's, Relief Society president's friend was brought into the Church by his wife before they were married." We've all heard similar stories. Sharing the gospel with nonmember friends and working to reactivate less active members are important — but this is work that can be accomplished within groups and families. Single dating is not prime time for missionary work. Not even missionaries attempt to teach the gospel to others one-on-one. They stay with companions.

As Latter-day Saints, we must stand up for the dating standards that set us apart. Rather than pushing against the fence and trying to be like everyone else, we must take advantage of the differences that make us unique. It is said that beloved author and illustrator Dr. Seuss was once criticized by a teacher who told him he should draw more like everyone else in his class. Two-headed creatures with multi-colored feathers growing out of their ears are not usually considered the norm. But how glad we are that Dr. Seuss did not cave in to the pressure to conform. Children all over the world will always be grateful that he was not afraid to be different from his classmates. We must have similar courage to keep our standards.

A STANDS FOR ATTITUDE

We can make even the "pittiest" dates and social interactions more positive experiences by having a good attitude. When I attend Church dances, I see the difference that attitude makes. Right in the same room some will say, "This is the best dance ever," while others will complain, "This is the worst." The music is exactly the same. Refreshments are identical. The lighting is the same. It is only the attitudes that differ. A positive attitude insures that we will enjoy the situation instead of feeling like it is a downer.

At a stake dance, gentlemen invite young women to dance. Girls that don't dance at dances are called wallflowers. Boys that don't dance at dances are called wall-weeds. Standing around with your buddies from the teachers quorum might make you feel a lot safer and keep you from having to put your ego on the line, but you are at the dance for social interaction. Change your attitude, and you will find it much easier to step outside your comfort zone and stop pretending you're there just to listen to the music.

Ladies, say "Yes," when you are invited to dance. You have no idea how much courage it takes for many of these young men to approach you.

He's been standing there, in the safety of a circle of his friends, trying to look inconspicuous. All the guys are pretending like they don't have any interest in dancing. But he's spotted this girl he wants to ask to dance. His heart is beating wildly, he feels a little breathless, and his hands get wet and clammy. Finally, he sucks in a big breath, and launches himself away from the safety of his group and takes an awkward walk across the floor, heading for the girl he has decided to ask. He hardly dares look at her, and he isn't sure his voice is going to work. But, somehow, he manages to say, "Do you want to dance?"

I've heard girls refuse to dance because, "I don't like the group that is playing this song." Hearing that, I have felt like saying, "I don't care if it's the Tabernacle Choir! Get out there and dance."

Another girl said, "No, my leg hurts."

I wanted to respond, "It *will* hurt when I'm through with you."

C'mon. Reward his courage. Have a heart! It doesn't matter if the guy asking is the biggest nerd you have ever seen and has two left feet. Smile, say, "Thank you," and then get out there and make him feel like a million bucks. Rather than standing on the dance floor making faces at your friends across the room, and acting like you're doing a service project for the kingdom, try focusing on the young man you are with and making him feel like he's important.

I know many girls are reluctant to try this. One young woman complained, "But, the minute you are nice to the little weirdo, he leeches on to you, and then he follows you around all night like a bad dream."

My friend Vivian Cline says that the rule is this: You must say yes — once. After that, you can tactfully say, "I've already had the chance to dance with you, and there are a lots of girls here tonight who need that chance."

I know about a young lady who was invited to the biggest and most formal dance of the year by a young man she wasn't excited to go with. Her father encouraged her to go.

"But Dad," she cried, "I just can't go with *him*."

Her father asked, "Is he over sixteen?"

"Yes."

"Will you be in a group doing something wholesome and worthwhile?"

"Yes."

"Is he a worthy priesthood holder?"

"Yes."

She knew her father was right. She ought to accept his invitation, at least this once. She struggled to overcome her reluctance, accepted the date, and tried to have a positive attitude about it. She made an effort to make the evening wonderful for her date, for the others she was with, and for herself. She was surprised how much fun she had. After the evening was over, and the boy called her again, she politely and legitimately said, "No, thank you."

But what happens, when you finally turn sixteen, if the phone doesn't ring? Then you turn seventeen, and the phone still doesn't ring? And now you're twenty-nine, and the phone still hasn't rung?

The advice remains the same. Keep a positive attitude. When that handsome guy comes running up to you on the dance floor and says thoughtlessly, "Hey, where's your sister?" think of what one of my high school teachers told me about lettuce and carrots.

If you are going into a store and you want to buy lettuce, it doesn't matter how fresh the carrots are. If you're looking for lettuce, it doesn't even matter if the carrots are on sale, or they are crisp, or if they have just been sprayed with the little mist. The desire you have for lettuce doesn't diminish the excellence of the carrots. It just means you are not in the market at that moment for carrots — lettuce is what you are looking for.

The next time you're feeling just a little bit rejected or passed over, think to yourself, "I'm a carrot. I'm an awesome carrot!" Then one day, someone is going to come into the store wanting carrots, and, believe me, it will not matter what the lettuce looks like. He'll come into the store for a carrot, and you'll be there.

Rejection is hard to take. But a positive attitude makes it possible to survive. I have a friend who was tapped to join a social club when she was in high school. After a week of initiation — having to come to school in her night robe, and in curlers, with shaving cream on her face — she was called before the big life-

and-death committee and told, "We're sorry, but you didn't make it."

This girl stood up straight, flipped her hair back, and said, "You lose!"

What goes for girls also goes for guys. Next time you get turned down for a dance or a date, keep that same positive outlook. Just flip your missionary haircut, and *think* (don't you dare say it), "You lose. You could have had *me*. But, you lose." That's a winning attitude.

T STANDS FOR TRUE

In all dating situations, be true to God, baptismal covenants, your parents' trust, and to yourself. Follow the promptings of the Holy Ghost.

One bishop expressed concern that fourteen- and fifteen-year-olds were coming to him with serious moral problems, but they felt like they were "okay" because they had never been on a formal date. They understood clearly that they should not date until they were sixteen, but, somehow, they felt justified in doing about anything else they wanted with members of the opposite sex, just as long as they didn't call their experiences together an official "date." Young people who pick and choose which standards they will keep, and who rationalize their poor choices by playing word games, will always end up the losers. They lose the Spirit, peace of mind, self-esteem, opportunities, and blessings. Happiness and joy are the consequences of adhering to God's commandments, not of finding ways around them.

I know of a returned missionary and his girl friend who started dating seriously. They enjoyed each other's company. And, before they knew it, they started to enjoy a few other things—things that are not legitimate until a couple is married. That's where they went wrong.

In the Garden of Eden, Adam and Eve were commanded not to partake of the fruit of the tree of knowledge of good and evil, but not because the fruit itself was bad. Whatever its merits—it was described as being "good for food . . . [and] pleasant to the eyes" (Moses 4:12) — its use was forbidden them. Moreover, they were warned of serious consequences if they chose to be disobedient to the commandment they had been given to not eat it.

Similarly, the Lord has commanded that we not trifle with or use our procreative powers until after we are married. He has warned us that disobedience will result in heartache, remorse, sorrow, and unwanted consequences. The suggestions given us by our church leaders are calculated to help us keep ourselves morally clean, and to avoid temptations we may not be able to resist.

E STANDS FOR EXCITING

Make your dates and social interactions memorable. Don't just call up and say, "What do you want to do?"

"I don't know. What do *you* want to do?"

"I don't know. I asked you first."

Have a plan in mind when you ask someone out. Make sure it is something fun and exciting — something that you and your date will both be able to get the most mileage out of when your future grandchildren ask you about the "good old days." The First Presidency has counseled youth to "Plan positive and constructive activities when you are together. Do things that help you get to know each other. Be careful to go to places where there is a good environment, where you won't be faced with temptation" (*For the Strength of Youth,* p. 7).

A group of young men once asked my wife to help them pull off a stunt they had planned for their dates. Debi is a nurse, and she works part time in the same-day surgery unit of a medical center. The gentlemen asked if she would wear her nurses uniform and serve dinner to them and their dates. Before serving the real dinner, they wanted my wife to "prep" the girls' arms, as she would before drawing blood. Then, instead of bringing out plates of food, she was to wheel out IV bottles. The guys hoped the girls would be puzzled, and would ask, "What's going on?" The guys would answer, "You've heard of TV dinners? These are IV dinners. This way we can each have our meal and still have a good conversation. Without having to chew, we won't have to worry about getting stuff in our teeth!"

My wife, who was happy to help them, laughed, and said, "You're doing it right. You're going to scare the girls to death! They'll remember this date!"

I know other creative young people who have played water baseball. First, second, and third bases were little wading pools, and home plate was a Slip-and-Slide. At one group date, each group was given a toothpick and challenged to come back at a certain time later that night with something bigger and better. At the end of the evening, these teenagers arrived at the meeting place dragging the most incredible collection of junk you can imagine. One group had an old motorcycle. Another had a rusty swing set. And one group even had a family! It's true, there they were: father, mother, kids, and a baby. Needless to say, the youth had a memorable evening because they made this date exciting.

D–A–T–E: As easily as we can spell the word, we can remember the importance of standing up for LDS *differences,* making social interactions great by our *attitudes,* being *true* to our moral values, and making our dates creative and *exciting.* Dates don't all have pits. Enjoy.

Brad Wilcox is on leave from his teaching assignment in the Elementary Education Department at Brigham Young University to work on his Ph.D. degree. Brad spent his childhood years in Ethiopia, and he has traveled all over the world. He is the author of four books and writes extensively for the Church magazines. Brother Wilcox enjoys journal writing and driving with his car radio turned way up, and is proud of his one-time appearance on TV's "Family Feud." He and his wife, Debi, have four children.

20

PROFANITY: "OUR WORDS WILL CONDEMN US"

RANDAL A. WRIGHT

In 1985 I attended a missionary farewell for my friend Eric. He and his sister, Heidi, had been the only members of the Church in a large Texas high school. I had assumed that these two young Latter-day Saint youth would have been a good example in their school, but I didn't realize how good, until I listened to Heidi's talk at the farewell. She said that a nonmember friend told her that Eric was the only boy she had ever known who never used profanity. Think about that for a moment — she had never known anyone who did not use bad language, until she met Eric. What an example to the school! I got a little emotional as I thought of this young man and the impression he'd made. I'm sure the Lord was very pleased with Eric.

A few years later, Tim Franklin, another Latter-day Saint from Texas, had the opportunity to play on his school's football team. Unlike the school Eric attended, Tim had the privilege of attending a high school with about eighty other LDS students. His three older brothers had preceded him as members of the football team, and had set good examples, before graduating and filling missions. One night Tim played in a hard-fought game, where emotions were running high. After one of the plays, Tim called out loudly to a teammate, whose name was Damion, to give him some instructions for the next play. When the referee heard Tim say "Damion," he threw his flag and penalized Tim for unsportsmanlike conduct. The official thought Tim had used a swear word. Tim tried to explain that he was not using profanity, but was just calling the name of one of his teammates. The referee refused to listen and marched off the long penalty against the team. When the explanation for the penalty reached the bench, Tim's teammates couldn't believe it. One player, who was known for his vulgar language, tried to convince the disbelieving official by saying, "Tim is a Mormon, and Mormon boys don't cuss."

I have often thought about that statement — "Mormon boys don't cuss." Is that true in your school? Is it true in your home? Is it true of you?

One day I asked my high-school-aged son to think of all the non-LDS youth who had never used profanity around him. He thought for a long time and finally named one boy and one girl. I then asked him to do the same for all the youth who were members of the Church. The names mentioned represented only a small number of the LDS students attending his school. He said that the rest used bad language just like the nonmembers.

A statement made by George Washington came to mind. The first president of our great country said, "The foolish and wicked practice of profane cursing and swearing is a vice so mean and low that every person of sense and character detests and despises it."

Why then do so many people in the world use this kind of language? How common is profanity? What are the consequences of its use, and how can we stop using it if we have a problem with it?

I recently asked my nephew Cory, who is a sophomore in high school, to count the profane words he heard at school in one day. That evening he invited me over to his house to give me his report. I found he had gone a little further with his profanity count than I had asked. He had not only counted the number of profane words heard that day, but he had also listed the first letter of each word on paper, then put them in order by the actual number of times each word was used. Although he didn't count before school, during lunch, or after school, his total came to 194 profane words used in his classrooms during the day!

The next day I stood in line for an hour and fifteen minutes at the university where I was teaching, waiting to pick up some basketball tickets. I did a similar profanity count while in line. One hundred fifteen profane words were used by those standing around me during that time period. It was interesting that the top three words on my list were the same as the top three on my nephew's list.

At almost every turn we hear language that is vulgar and profane. Language that used to be called "talk of sailors" is now the jargon of our communities, schools, and even our homes. Young women have now joined in, and are using language that would have been thought scandalous in previous generations. Teachers throughout the United States are complaining that even pre-school-aged children are using vulgar language.

The common use of profanity and vulgarity is spreading like a plague across our society. Many members of the Church don't even seem to realize the offensive nature of this kind of language. Some attempt to justify its use by saying, "everyone is doing it." And while it's true that the use of profanity is very common in our society, this kind of language is unbecoming and wrong, no matter how common the practice becomes.

Have you ever wondered why the use of profanity is increasing at such an alarming rate in our society? How do people from Texas to New York, and from California to Florida, know which four-letter words to use? There are many factors involved in its spread. We are hearing it used more in our schools, in our communities, by our friends, and even increasingly by our teachers. Parents are also using it in their homes. And the media does much to promote the use of profanity — especially movies and television. I recently did an analysis of every movie released in the first six months of 1992. Using the information in the *Entertainment Research Report*, a movie content fact sheet, I found the following data on profanity:

Percent of movies containing profanity			Average number of profane words per movie	
R	64 of 64	100%	R	73
PG-13	29 of 30	97%	PG-13	31
PG	18 of 20	90%	PG	16
G	0 of 3	00%	G	0
Total:	111 of 117	95%	Average:	50

If you had seen all the movies that played during the first six months of 1992, you would have heard a total of 5,907 vulgar or profane words. That is an overall average of 50 per movie, or about one vulgar word every two minutes. It's not quite as bad as Bob Hope said, but it's getting close. He said, "With today's movies, if we took out all the bad language, we'd go back to silent films." (*Reader's Digest,* August 1991, p. 130.)

What four letter word do you think is used most often in these recent films? It is a repulsive word that begins with the letter F and describes sexual relations in a degrading way. It was used 1,533 times in the movies analyzed, or, on average, over twelve times per movie. In one recent movie, not included in the above analysis, the word was used 308 times!

Research was recently conducted to discover which four-letter words the youth in America use most frequently. The number one and number two words used among teenagers were the same two used most in the movies. Do you think the script writers asked American youth which words they used so they could put them in the movie scripts? I don't think so. With enough exposure, youth begin talking like the media heroes they admire.

How could anyone sit and listen to these words over and over without being affected? Sterling W. Sill said: "We are training ourselves to love sin. We pay money to see it being committed on the screen, . . . and quite naturally we absorb it into our lives" (*Conference Report,* October 1964, p. 111). Surely the increase in the amount of profanity we are exposed to in the media is related somehow to its increased use in our society.

WHAT ARE THE CONSEQUENCES?

Can you think of any advantages that come from profaning the holy name of God or using degrading and crude language? I have tried to do so, but have discovered no benefit whatsoever. Now, see if you can think of any evil consequences that come from using inappropriate language? Many think that there is no harm in it. Our leaders, however, teach that this is not the case. Let's briefly look at some of the consequences of using profanity:

1. *Degrades and Destroys Souls*

President Joseph Fielding Smith: "Profanity is filthiness. A person is known as much by his language as he is by the company he keeps.... Filthiness in any form is degrading and soul-destroying and should be avoided" (*Doctrines of Salvation* [Salt Lake City: Bookcraft, 1954], 1:13).

2. *Diminishes Virtue*

President Ezra Taft Benson: "How can any man indulge himself in the evils of pornography, profanity, or vulgarity and consider himself totally virtuous?" ("Godly Characteristics of the Master," *Ensign*, November 1986, p. 46).

3. *Defiles Those Who Speak It*

President Gordon B. Hinckley: "Stay out of the gutter in your conversation. Foul talk defiles the man who speaks it.... Don't swear. Don't profane. Avoid so-called dirty jokes. Stay away from conversation that is sprinkled with foul and filthy words. You will be happier if you do so, and your example will give strength to others" ("Take Not the Name of God in Vain," *Ensign*, November 1987, pp. 47-48).

4. *Drives Out the Spirit of Reverence*

President David O. McKay: "Swearing is a vice that bespeaks a low standard of breeding. Blasphemous exclamations drive out all spirit of reverence" (*Gospel Ideals*, [Salt Lake City: The Improvement Era, 1970], p. 420).

5. *Is Called a Gross Sin*

The First Presidency: "The habit . . . , which some young people fall into, of using vulgarity and profanity . . . is not only offensive to well-bred persons, but it is a gross sin in the sight of God, and should not exist among the children of the Latter-day Saints" (Quoted by Gordon B. Hinckley, "Take Not the Name of God in Vain," *Ensign,* November 1987, p. 46).

6. *Destroys Mankind*

President Hugh B. Brown, speaking of Satan's weapons: "Lucifer uses all of them, even the secret thoughts of the mind and unclean conversation, as weapons in his arsenal to destroy mankind." ("Purity is Power," Tri-stake BYU Fireside, 1962, p. 22).

THE ORIGIN OF PROFANITY:

The importance of avoiding profanity becomes evident when we realize where it originates. To determine this, consider the subject matter of most profanity. Profanity is a perversion of any of four sacred topics: (1) the names or titles of Deity; (2) sexual relations; (3) the body and its functions; (4) human relationships. Given the sanctity of each of these things, can there be any doubt about who is the author of vulgar perversions of them? Seen in this light, it is easy to understand why profanity is so offensive to the Lord. Let's take a closer look at each of these.

1. *Taking the Lord's name in vain*

It is probably safe to say that the commandment most often broken in this world is, "Thou shalt not take the name of the Lord thy God in vain; for the Lord will not hold him guiltless that taketh his name in vain" (Exodus 20:7). Have you ever wondered why the Lord gave such a commandment? Consider this:

When was the last time you heard Satan referred to in a derogatory way? That does not seem to happen. But, when was the last time you heard the name of the Lord being taken in vain? It should be clear that it is the adversary who is served by profane references to Deity. Satan is angry with God and his Only Begotten Son, and it must please the devil when God's children refer to the Father and the Son disrespectfully; particularly when that disrespect is coupled with angry expressions of vulgarity. We become Satan's emissaries and agents if we endorse the hatred he harbors for Heavenly Father and Jesus, by misusing their sacred names. Taking the Lord's name in vain shows a fundamental disrespect for spiritual things, and the practice can destroy our relationship with Heavenly Father. For instance, how can a person curse something in the name of the Lord and then presume to pray with humility and reverence to the same Being? Surely, a person who blasphemes the name of his or her Maker creates a distance between them. Then too, the use of profanity often leads a person into the company of the corrupt. And if people show this kind of disrespect toward their creator, aren't they also likely to ignore other commandments and commit other sins as well?

One of our modern-day special witnesses of the Savior has said, "There are no more sacred or significant words in all of our language than the names of God the Father and his Son, Jesus Christ. . . . Satan seeks to discredit the sacred names of God the Father and his Son, Jesus Christ, the names through which their work is done. He succeeds in a measure whenever he is able to influence any man or woman, boy or girl, to make holy names common and to associate them with coarse thoughts and evil acts. Those who use sacred names in vain are, by that act, promoters of Satan's purposes" (Dallin H. Oaks, "Reverent and Clean," *Ensign,* May 1986, pp. 50–51).

Here again, the movie and television industry are among the biggest offenders. In a study done in 1986, I found ninety-two profane references to Deity during a week of prime-time television programming (7 PM to 10 PM) on the three major network stations. By 1992, the number of profane references to Deity during a sample week of prime-time television had climbed to 158. The movies released during the first six months of 1992 included 1,126 profane references to Deity, or an average of almost ten per movie. Why would an industry include such references when a vast majority of Americans claim to believe in God? Or, maybe a better question is, why do people submit to listening to their God being profaned?

Not only should we not take the Lord's name in vain, we should do all in our power to encourage others not to do it either. I am reminded of an event in the life of President Spencer W. Kimball regarding this subject. He was very ill when he had this experience: "In the hospital one day I was wheeled out of the operating room by an attendant who stumbled, and there issued from his angry lips vicious cursing with a combination of the names of the Savior. Even half-conscious, I recoiled and implored: 'Please! Please! That is my Lord whose name you revile.' There was a deathly silence, then a subdued voice whispered: 'I am sorry' " ("Profane Not the Name of Thy God!" *Improvement Era*, May 1953, p. 320).

2. *Describing sexual relations*

By blessing us with the power to have children, the Lord has entrusted men and women with the ability to participate with him in the creation process. That sacred power is only to be used by married couples, and should even then be treated reverently. We have been told that in the eternities it will only be extended to those who reach the highest degree of the celestial kingdom (see D&C 132:19). Seen in this light, can you imagine the sorrow that our loving Father must feel when his children prostitute this gift, or make it the subject of lewd stories? It is difficult to imagine anything more offensive to Heavenly Father than to label the procreative act with ugly, four-letter words — more so when those words are used in the context of cursing one another. There is no way we can justify making the sexual relationship the subject of cheap talk and vulgar expressions.

3. *Describing body parts and functions*

One of the main purposes of our coming to earth is to obtain a body. It is a sacred temple, provided by our Father, to be gratefully used in our attempt to work out our salvation. The prophet Joseph Smith taught, "We came to this earth that we might have a body and present it pure before God in the celestial kingdom. The great principle of happiness consists in having a body. The devil has no body, and herein is his punishment. . . . When cast out by the Savior he asked to go into the herd of swine, showing that he would prefer a swine's body to having none. All beings who have bodies have power over those who have not" (*Teachings of the Prophet Joseph Smith* [Salt Lake City: The Deseret News Press, 1938], p. 181).

Imagine how it pleases Satan when mortals refer to body parts and functions in degrading ways. He is jealous of us and our mortal bodies, and wants to destroy us. He is miserable, and wants others to be miserable like he is. He succeeds somewhat in his purposes when he can get us to use language that in any way demeans the sacred human body.

4. *Degrading people*

The scriptures teach that "on these two commandments hang all the law and the prophets" (Matthew 22:40). The two laws are to love God, and to love your neighbor. We must love one another to be happy. Indeed, it is one of our greatest needs as human beings — to be loved and valued. And so, it is not entirely true to say that "names can never hurt us." The fact is that mean-spirited and vulgar criticisms have the power to wound our feelings, and rob us of our self-esteem and confidence. How disappointed the Lord must be when he hears one of his children mocking and cursing another through cheap language and vulgar names.

It is not hard to imagine profanity being used among the inmates of a state penitentiary. In fact, I'm convinced that some of the most filthy of all language is spoken among those who are at odds with the laws of the land. Things haven't changed much since the New Testament days of Peter who spoke of the "filthy conversation of the wicked" (2 Peter 2:7). Filthy conversation is still associated with wickedness.

Try to imagine Jesus Christ or his angels using profanity. No, that isn't possible. The Nephites heard Jesus speak and pray for them and described the experience with these words: "And no tongue can speak, neither can there be written by any man, neither can the hearts of men conceive so great and marvelous things as we both saw and heard Jesus speak; and no one can conceive of the joy which filled our souls at the time we heard him pray for us unto the Father" (3 Nephi 17:18).

In our dispensation Oliver Cowdery described the experience of hearing an angel of God speak by saying, "I shall not attempt to paint to you the feelings of this heart, nor the majestic beauty and glory which surrounded us on this occasion; but you will believe me when I say, that earth, nor men, with the eloquence of time, cannot begin to clothe language in as interesting and sublime a manner as this holy personage" (*Messenger and Advocate,* vol. 1 [October 1834], pp. 14–16; see also footnote to Joseph Smith–History 1:71).

At baptism, all of us covenanted that we would take upon us the name of Christ. That is, we would try to do what he would do in any given situation. If neither Christ nor his holy angels would use profanity, then obviously, neither should we.

While attending Brigham Young University, I took a very interesting class in youth leadership. The class was held right before dinner time, and we were usually hungry during the lecture. One day my professor brought in a beautiful cake and placed it on his desk in front of the class. I can't tell you how good it looked and how much I wanted a piece.

During the class period he talked about how we present ourselves to others. He emphasized that it matters *how* things are presented. I didn't think that much about his point until the class came to a close. He asked how many of us wanted a piece of cake. Almost every hand in the class went up. He gave each of us a paper plate and a spoon. I was so excited. Then as he came to each desk, he put his hand in the cake, picked up a piece, squeezed it between his fingers, and dumped it onto our plate. It almost made me sick as I watched that beautiful cake being ruined. When he finished giving everyone a glob of what had been a beautiful cake, he returned to the front of the room, looked at the class, and said, "You see, it does matter how things are presented." I will never forget that lesson. I think it has application for all of us.

It does matter how we present ourselves to others. Few things can ruin our good image more than filthy words coming from our lips. Our words reflect the kind of people we are, reveal our beliefs, and define us for the people who observe us.

One day we will stand at the judgment bar and answer for all our words and thoughts, whether they have been good or evil.

Alma cautioned us: "For our words will condemn us, yea, all our works will condemn us; we shall not be found spotless; and our thoughts will also condemn us; and in this awful state we shall not dare to look up to our God; and we would fain be glad if we could command the rocks and the mountains to fall upon us to hide us from his presence" (Alma 12:14).

Let's make a new resolve to live a clean life, and let our words be positive and free from the filthy language of our day. Then, instead of our judgment being a fearful experience, it will be one of happiness and joy.

What can a person do to break the vile and filthy habit of using profanity? There *are* ways to change this kind of behavior. Some people make a deal with a friend that they will fine themselves a certain amount of money for every inappropriate word they speak. But I believe the most effective way to eliminate profanity from our speech is to fast and pray for help. On the day of the fast, find a quiet place where you can sit and ponder. Take out a piece of paper and write at the top, "Things I Can Do to Break the Habit of Profanity." Once you have written the heading, sit and ponder the possibilities. As thoughts come into your mind, write them down. This will be personal revelation to you from the Lord. Once you have recorded the ideas, review them frequently, and pray for the strength to do what the Lord has revealed to you.

If this is a habit you need to break, you can do it! You can eliminate profanity and vulgarity from your speech, and one day return to your Father in Heaven clean and pure. I challenge you to begin this very day.

Randal A. Wright is an instructor of Religion at Brigham Young University. He has previously served as a coordinator and director of Seminaries and Institutes. Randal is the author of Protecting Your Family in an X-Rated World, *and he was the founder and editor of* Mormon Sport Magazine. *Brother Wright lists his interests as speaking to youth, going to waterparks, playing and watching basketball, reading autobiographies, and listening to country/Western music. He and his wife, Wendy, have five children.*